HOW TO BE
A POLICE OFFICER

HOW TO BE
A POLICE OFFICER

GRAHAM WETTONE

Biteback Publishing

First published in Great Britain in 2017 by
Biteback Publishing Ltd
Westminster Tower
3 Albert Embankment
London SE1 7SP
Copyright © Graham Wettone 2017

Graham Wettone has asserted his right under the Copyright, Designs and
Patents Act 1988 to be identified as the author of this work.

ISBN 978-1-78590-219-2

10 9 8 7 6 5 4 3 2 1

A CIP catalogue record for this book is available from the British Library.

Set in Adobe Garamond Pro and Gill Sans by Adrian McLaughlin

Printed and bound in Great Britain by
CPI Group (UK) Ltd, Croydon CR0 4YY

CONTENTS

This book is dedicated firstly to my mum, who passed
away in 2008, for her inspiration, selfless commitment and
dedication when raising me mostly on her own. She instilled
in me the values, honesty and work ethic that have sustained
me in my life and policing career. I owe her everything and
miss her daily. She would have been so proud of this.

Secondly, and equally as importantly, I dedicate this to
everyone who ever worked or hopes to work on
'the thin blue line'. Thank you for all you
have done, are doing and will do. The police
became my family and will always remain so.

CHAPTER 1

WHY DO YOU WANT TO BE
A POLICE OFFICER?

The first thing you need to ask yourself is 'Why?' Of all the professions and occupations you can embark upon, why on earth in this day and age would any sane, sensible and balanced individual consider becoming a police officer? The recent murder of PC Keith Palmer highlights the dangers that officers face every day whilst policing the streets of Britain. This devastating tragedy, along with the deaths of PC Keith Blakelock, PC Yvonne Fletcher, PC Dave Phillips and others, demonstrates the ultimate risks of the job; and sadly, such risks are unlikely to go away.

The police service, or force as some still like to call it, seems to be constantly criticised for current or alleged historical errors – and this blame culture will also apply to you whether you joined thirty years ago or thirty minutes ago. You will be held responsible for every mismanaged major crime scene and inquiry, every public disaster or protest that arguably went wrong and every perceived miscarriage of justice. That is not to say that the police have not made some monumental errors over the last forty years. I served as an operational officer, and I hasten to add that I was not involved in, or even present at, almost all of them! You should be prepared for the reality that the errors and organisational mistakes made by the entire police service will be deposited at your feet by someone, somewhere, at some time.

The police do seem to attract headlines for mistakes more than any other organisation and in my opinion, there is a good reason for it. The first thing you need to understand is the fundamental principle of British policing, which is that we police by public consent. This is a phrase that you will hear throughout your time in the police and it is essential you understand and apply it every day you work as a police officer in the UK. It means that the police protect and serve the public and can do so because the vast majority of the public fully support their police service. It is for this reason that any mistake made by the police is thoroughly examined, arguably in finer detail than errors made by those in any other profession, and questions are asked of the police to justify all their actions and decisions. Before you embark upon a career in policing, you should know that at some stage you may be asked to account for an error that had nothing to do with you personally, but you may be viewed by the very public you protect as guilty by association. Once you wear the uniform or carry a warrant card, you are considered partly responsible for policing as a whole. The public demands the best from their police service and deserves honest and forthright answers when the police get things wrong; although regrettably, this has not always been the case, as several high-profile cases have shown.

So, as a police officer, what can you expect and what may noticeably change in your everyday life? Every armchair expert will make a beeline for you in pubs and at parties and ask for your view on Hillsborough, the Lawrence inquiry and any other high-profile case considered as being far from the police's finest hour. The moment you join the police, some may label you with that well-worn title 'institutionally racist', just by virtue of holding the office of constable. Well, that's certainly how the Metropolitan Police is perceived, but it's also now generally assumed of anyone wearing the uniform. This stigma came from the Macpherson inquiry into the Stephen Lawrence murder and has been regularly repeated over the years in a number of cases and topics.

I grew up in south London and attended a diverse comprehensive school. I have never considered myself racist, just a 'criminalist' who loathes all bullies. I worked as a uniformed front-line officer in 1993 and I spent my working days seeking out active criminals in the area and doing my best to disrupt and detain them to prevent them committing crime. It mattered not a jot what ethnicity or background they were from. My colleagues and I only cared that they were committing crime.

Policing now serves a large area and so there is a clear need for the police to represent the community. The police service itself is now more diverse than ever before. You will work alongside people from all sorts of backgrounds and beliefs and you will undoubtedly forge close friendships with many of them. It is inconceivable then that you will not change in many ways by virtue of what you encounter at work and who you work with. Like all walks of life and professions, you take something from every person you meet, including your parents, friends, family and work colleagues.

Policing has changed over the decades since I joined, and those thinking of starting their careers now have to ask themselves, 'What sort of police officer do I want to be?' There have been some officers who have behaved wrongly, poorly and occasionally criminally, but they are in the minority and generally despised by the majority who just want to do their job well. You will hopefully follow the good example of diligent colleagues around you. You cannot just teach policing from a book or an online training package; new officers need to watch and learn from experienced police officers to observe different ways or methods of working. Ask yourself what sort of officer you want to be and then learn from those around you – or find a good book that tells you how to be a police officer!

When you answer the dreaded question, 'What do you do, then?' with 'Oh, I'm a police officer', the facial expression of your new-found friend or potential romantic partner will usually change and you will no doubt hear all about their speeding ticket that was 'unfair' or 'way too harsh', or the fine for using a mobile phone when it wasn't really their fault or the phone wasn't being used … 'I was just reading a text!' As it happens, very few police officers refer to themselves as being a cop and usually say instead that they are in 'the job'. This isn't just a euphemism to avoid complaints – for many current or retired police officers, 'the job' is the only one they've ever really wanted.

No matter how much an officer loves their job, however, be under no false illusions here. The incidents and things you will be called upon to deal with are possibly the most terrible things you can see in society. You will be exposed to the very worst in some people and will witness some truly awful scenes. On many occasions, you cannot go home and honestly answer the question from your loved ones and family, 'Did you have a good day at work?' The words to answer that simple question repeated in many other households across the country do not come so easily for many police officers. As terrible as it can be, however, you may well find some previously hidden inner strength and courage in yourself whilst dealing with the most shocking situations. You will astonish yourself with what you can cope with, although the training and the camaraderie of your fellow officers will help to support you. Policing will change you and you will develop a kind of hardness and resilience to face problems and people. A more decisive nature and confidence will grow within you as you gain experience and deal with all kinds of challenging situations.

People deal with stress or challenges in many different ways and, in general, police officers will use a form of humour to alleviate their feelings. This is often not the type of humour that can be understood by those outside policing or any of the other emergency services. Expect very little sympathy from your colleagues after dealing with your third suicide or similar traumatic incident in a month. Those types of incidents seem to come along like buses, usually three or four at once. I can remember having to report four suicides as a result of hanging within the space of six months whilst working in south London. My helpful colleagues dubbed me 'Albert' for a short while after the well-known hangman Albert Pierrepoint, and I also heard several comments like, 'You just hanging around the canteen today?' or, 'How about you *swing* past the station for a tea later?' You know, the sort of things with a hidden meaning. No comforting arm around my shoulder or a concerned colleague asking if I was feeling OK or if I needed a chat. The attitude back then was you just got on with the job and if you showed a lack of confidence or courage, it was seen as a sign of weakness. Fortunately, things have improved to a degree in current policing and far more is done to provide welfare and support for officers involved in traumatic incidents, but the service as a whole could still do with providing better support systems.

I attended all four of those incidents on my own due to the low number of officers on my team. Dwindling numbers was an issue in the '80s and it was common to patrol alone. This changed for a while afterwards, but it seems that policing has re-invented the wheel by making single patrol the default option once again, with many forces now opting for single-crewed vehicles. This means that in many parts of the UK, the front-line officers will patrol by themselves, and you may well see the much-loved *Dixon of Dock Green* iconic image of a single officer walking along the road. The imagery of PC George Dixon from the film *Blue Light* is one which many people still hanker after, even though he was shot dead fairly early on in the film. This 1960s cop was resurrected and given his own show on the BBC which started and ended with a cheery 'Evening, all' before racing you through the policing he faced and solved in an hour. A very entertaining film (aside from when he was shot dead!) and a great TV series, and although it is far from the real life of policing and PC Dixon is not exactly a model for doing the job properly, it inspired many a young person to join. But back to walking the beat alone. In order to have officers patrolling together on foot, the remaining officers must patrol in the cars on their own, so as a police officer you may have to accept some lonely times at work.

I am a vociferous objector to single-crewing and would argue that it is hugely counterproductive. It's also worth noting that it is usually proposed by those who have never actually driven a police car on their own. As it is, if you are considering a policing career, you and your family should consider that you may end up walking the streets late at night or driving a response car on your own. Should that put you off? I really hope not and any risky calls that you are deployed to will attract support from your colleagues, as it is likely they would want you to do the same for them.

Some people like working solo and you may even consider when you look around the briefing room that you would prefer to be alone than saddled with some of your colleagues. Policing can attract some interesting characters, although they do seem to be becoming less quirky as time passes. I worked with a few you could describe as being mildly eccentric or just plain odd. I worked with a lovely bloke called Vic in the early '90s who thought he was a better left-back than police officer – which was possibly the case, although he spent more time on the subs bench in a tracksuit than playing any football! I was occasionally posted with him driving the Wimbledon area car, Victor One, on early turn and this is where I discovered his peculiar party-piece. Vic had a problem with early mornings and alarm clocks, which was a challenge for a shift worker. This meant he was habitually late and looked like he had been dragged through a hedge backwards on the rare occasion when he did make it to work at 6 a.m., although it was more like 7 a.m. when he eventually arrived. After waiting for him to turn up as my radio operator, his first port of call was always the colloquial trap one (toilet) downstairs, after which he took delight in explaining to me what had passed (literally) in great detail. As I drove the sleek Rover SD1 around the streets of Wimbledon, the only respite I had from this pre-breakfast narrative was his demand that we 'pop up' to the village so he could collect his morning paper. Vic considered himself an educated man so he always read the *Daily Telegraph* whenever he was in public, although in private he was definitely a *Sun* man. If you have ever tried to read the *Daily Telegraph* on your morning commute, you will already guess the problem we then faced. I am driving a marked police car around looking for crime, whilst sitting next to me is a six-foot tall bloke with a broadsheet newspaper fully open, reading it out loud. Half of my windscreen would disappear under his demand for current affairs, along with any view of my nearside wing mirror.

He steadfastly refused to do any work until he had read the paper – but that wasn't the best bit. His real pièce de résistance came from his nose. Vic had obviously not had time to fully complete his morning routine so he often sat next to me sniffling and snorting and complaining that his nose was blocked. He would then remove the obstruction from his nasal cavity and, with a degree of pride, place said object on the dashboard and admire it like some kind of trophy. By the time we returned to the station for our breakfast at 10.30 a.m., my dashboard was lined with several objects Vic had removed from his nose whilst reading the *Telegraph*. I sometimes thought his nose defied all medical reasoning – a mystery akin to the Bermuda Triangle – looking at what came out of it during the morning. Breakfast on those days was always a challenge, proving that, on occasion, single crewing can be a relief!

Having said all that, once he had visited trap one, read his paper, cleared his nasal cavity and generally woken up (usually around 11.30 a.m.), he was a good cop and the afternoon patrol was fun and he knew his villains very well. He made up for doing little or nothing in the first half of the shift by excelling in the latter, and we had some decent arrests and jobs together.

Maybe he was a decent left-back after all, but only after half-time and coming on as a sub!

There surely must be some kind of upside for police officers though, and there are indeed hugely rewarding aspects of the job. This job is at its best when you feel a great degree of loyalty, a very strong bond and deep friendship with the people you work with. Whilst Vic and I are still good friends (although I don't invite him round to my house before midday!), it doesn't mean you will become bosom buddies with every colleague you end up sharing a patrol car with for eight hours. There will be times when you possibly cannot stand your assigned partner for the day and they may have the odd annoying habit or, even worse, a really bad case of bad breath or body odour. I have worked with a few like that and occasionally the odd hint or comment may enlighten them, but with some you have to take a more direct approach. A deodorant can or a tube of toothpaste left in their correspondence tray sometimes does the trick!

So, there are some bonuses for single patrolling. But largely and ideally you should be paired up with another officer. A popular misconception that has been created by many police TV shows is that you have a permanent partner in policing, someone you are paired with every working day and, in TV world, they often seem to be best friends. They visit each other's houses, know their inner-most secrets and spend every waking moment alongside each other even when not at work. In the real policing world that is not the reality and, although there are some deployments for which you will be paired with another officer, they don't last for any significant period of time. As a police sergeant in the late '90s who was responsible for the postings and deployments of my team, I can safely say that it was usually the most difficult task of the day. You need to know the officers and how they work very well, something that is far easier said than done. As with all walks of life, there are always people you get on with better than others. There are those you would not want to be stuck in a lift with for more than a minute, let alone inside a police response car for eight to twelve hours – unless you have a peculiar interest in the contents of their nasal cavity!

It is the job of the supervisors to consider which vehicles and tasks need to be covered for each shift or tour of duty, and allocate the resources or the police officers available to oversee those tasks. I can still remember the anticipation and, at times, sheer dread of my team as I read out the postings for the day, who was in which vehicle and who they would be working alongside for that shift. There is a balance between putting people together who get on and work well together, and sharing the less-welcome postings. You can be sure that each officer keeps a personal tally of the times they have been posted with such-and-such, and they will remind you quite vocally that it's not their turn. This all comes down to basic people skills, and you will know how it works from your own experiences with classmates or work colleagues you have not really got on or worked well with. It's the same in policing, but what is different is that you must be able to trust your colleagues implicitly to do their job professionally and to be capable of supporting you at an incident. You may not like everyone you work with and the last thing you want to do is have them at your wedding or child's christening, but you need to be confident that their training and capability are sufficient to do the job when called upon.

What is it, then, that has attracted you to a police career, a job that is so readily criticised by some yet to this day is loved by most? For me, strangely enough, it was a TV show from the mid-70s still repeated on one of those gold channels, called *The Sweeney*. I was fifteen-and-a-half with no real idea what I wanted to do, helping out the local milkman at the weekends. My mum told me I had to start thinking about work after school and, in those days, not as many people took the university route and I was left in no doubt that I would have to find a job if I chose to leave school at sixteen. I was raised by my mum after my parents separated when I was eight and I can remember her having three jobs at once just to make ends meet. My desire to get on and work hard outside of the classroom was clearly hereditary. At sixteen, I was far more eager to leave school and start working for real, but the difficulty I faced was trying to decide what sort of career I wanted. My passion in life was football, but I realised in my early school years that I was unlikely to be good enough to make a career of it. I did play alongside a couple of people who went on to become professional footballers and one even captained Chelsea, the team I supported; but, despite several summers in his company, his skill and ability did not rub off on me. It did lead to some interesting chats over the next few years whenever I policed Chelsea games, as he would jog over during the warm up for a handshake and quick hello. It always went down well with the supporters to see their team captain smiling and joking with one of the local constabulary and greeting him like a long-lost friend!

My weekend job with our local milkman meant that from the age of thirteen I was up and out of the house by 6.30 a.m. most Saturday mornings, delivering the doorstep pint and collecting the weekly milk bill. I am not suggesting that every prospective police officer needs to become a milkman's helper, but it did give me valuable skills when it came to being able to communicate with people and it helped me to experience the already very diverse community in south London. My ambition by the time I was fifteen was to leave school at sixteen and become a milk-man, which I am sure filled my mum with some dread as I was at a very good school and doing quite well academically.

I am not sure when there was a definitive change in my mind, but at some point in 1976 I became fascinated by *The Sweeney*. Based on Scotland Yard's Flying Squad and their cockney rhyming slang nickname (the Sweeney from *Sweeney Todd*, which is the accepted rhyming slang for Flying Squad), they seemed to have an incredibly exciting working life. In those days, *The Sweeney* seemed to me to be a true representation of real life and, with no social media or 24-hour news coverage, there was little to disprove the assumption that what was on the screen was true to life.

I loved the fact they drove big, fast cars, usually Ford Granadas, fitted with sirens and a 3-litre engine, around the streets of London. They seemingly never had a moment to spare, but always solved the crime within the hour. I even recognised the scenes as they filmed many episodes in Fulham, and I was born in Parsons Green and both Mum and Dad's families lived around the area. It never occurred to me at that stage that I could end up working in a part of London I didn't know… like the north or east! I started to think about being a police officer, but didn't have a clue about how you'd even go about applying to join or what the job really involved. Surely I could just apply and then drive the flying squad around in their fast car with the sirens on?

Unbeknown to me at the time I was considering becoming a police officer, it was actually in my blood. My grandad on my father's side had been a special constable based at Fulham police station in the late 1920s. Life is indeed strange as some thirty years later, I would be working as a police sergeant based in Fulham, no doubt walking along the same corridors as my grandad had before me. This all came out after my application had been accepted, as my grandfather had died when my dad was only eighteen months old, so I knew very little about him or his life. Mum seized upon this teenage interest in being a police officer with vigour and, being a confident and forceful lady, she contacted the Metropolitan Police to find out more about joining. My mum would have made an excellent detective with her inquisitive mind and probing interview style, although sadly not all of her talents were hereditary. Despite my love of TV detective shows, I never fancied the real-life version and remained a uniformed officer throughout my service. One November night in 1976 we had a home visit by a police officer from the careers section and, suffice to say, it went well and they answered enough of my questions to convince me that policing was the job for me – although it sounded like I may have to wait a while before I got the keys to my Ford Granada. I was accepted into the then Metropolitan Police cadet corps, which was a residential training establishment located on the famous Hendon police training site, renowned the world over for its recruit, driver and detective training schools.

In truth, at such a young age I never really considered why I wanted to join beyond the fast cars and free work clothes. I never went through any form of decision-making process or considered my future career progression or earning potential. If I had, I am not sure policing would have come out anywhere near the top, as neither the wages nor the prospects were that great.

I certainly didn't consider the danger I would find myself in. Little did I know then that I would have petrol bombs thrown at me within two years of joining in one of the worst cases of civil disorder the UK mainland had ever seen in Brixton in 1981.

CHAPTER 2

IS IT DANGEROUS?

I will ask the obvious question: 'Is it dangerous?' Of course it is, and hopefully you have already worked that out for yourself before considering policing as a career. The anger, frustration and hostility in any confrontational situation alone show just how risky a job it can be. Police officers have no special psychic powers and receive no training in special martial arts, so they don't become a sort of uniformed super-hero capable of deflecting blows or assaults upon appointment. Whilst police officers will receive some fairly basic self-defence training together with guidance on using their personal protective equipment (PPE), they are still just human beings.

Officers are issued with a variety of equipment and pieces of approved kit to aid their self-defence, including the protective vest, which is capable of stopping a bullet from most hand-guns and also a blow from a knife. Next, there is the baton. The actual type varies from force to force, but most have a friction-lock baton, a steel implement which is initially about 6 inches long but extends to approximately 18 inches. There are other types of baton issued to forces across the UK, including an acrylic one which is made of one piece of hardened plastic, is solid and circular in shape and can be up to 24 inches in length. The next item is the incapacitant spray, which is usually a variant of CS spray or possibly pepper spray and is designed to be sprayed at any assailant to render them temporarily incapacitated so the officer can gain control of the situation. Another piece of equipment which some seem not to realise is part of the officers' PPE is the personal-issue handcuffs. In most forces now, they are the rigid type with a cuff at each end of a plastic-covered metallic centre piece, making it a single and non-flexible unit. The handcuff design was changed to this one-piece variety as it enables greater control of a suspect once you have managed to apply one half of the handcuff. It allows you to apply greater force by holding the centre part of the handcuff and then pulling or twisting the whole unit to gain control of the suspect. Some forces still have the old 'bracelet' style where the two parts of the handcuff are linked by a chain, meaning both cuffs are loose and flexible like the type found in most children's police play-sets. Lastly, for the majority of operational front-line officers, there is the Taser. It is currently only issued to selected officers who undergo specific and additional training in its use. It fires two barbed probes into the assailant and sends an electric shock through their system. At the time of writing, there are increased calls for Tasers to be issued far more widely and some are even asking for it to become standard issue for all officers.

The problem with most of these items is you need to be fairly close to the suspect to use them effectively. For example, when applying handcuffs you need to have hold of the person first. The newer rigid style allows you to apply what is called 'pain compliance', where at least one cuff is placed on the wrists of a suspect. Any movement of the rigid handcuff by the officer applying it will cause pain to the wrist where the cuff is applied. This was a new innovation when the design was first changed, as previously they were used primarily as a restraining measure to detain violent or escaping suspects. There is now extensive training in the correct way to apply handcuffs as all officers always have to justify any use of handcuffs.

When I first joined in 1979 there were no issue-handcuffs and, unbelievably, only one set of handcuffs for all the officers in each policing area. Back then, the only set of handcuffs was in the glove box of the one area car per borough and you had to sign for receipt of them when you started each shift. We also had no caged vans to transport violent suspects and so we could only handcuff assailants behind their back if we were very lucky.

Nowadays, caged vans and equipment to deal with extremely violent detainees are standard-issue. They even have leg restraints so you can tie up any violent person resisting arrest. Some forces now even have to use spit guards due to suspects spitting at officers and the associated risk of disease this carries. I find it abhorrent that a person would intentionally spit on someone else's face and hope the courts take the appropriate action, but it's yet another way in which you can find yourself in danger as a police officer. This additional equipment may seem frightening but, as with all the tactics, they are all reactionary measures and are only used to meet a specific threat posed by the person you are dealing with. The first positive action is usually started by the individual and the police officer then decides what reaction suits the threat they face.

Why do we need these additional pieces of equipment and does this mean that people have become more violent? Figures released in 2017 show that violent crime rose in 2016 with a 13–14 per cent increase of gun and knife crime. There was a reported 10 per cent rise in robberies and a 35 per cent rise in Public Order-related offences, which encompasses disorderly and violent behaviour incidents. These figures tend to support the overall view held by many serving officers that violent offences are on the rise. Police officers need adequate training and equipment to deal with these increases and protect themselves whilst doing so. It does seem that persons being arrested appear to have become less compliant and are more willing to resist arrest; and whilst these dangers warrant additional protective equipment, it is extremely important that modern officers don't become too reliant on their equipment. Some may argue that the additional kit and equipment has contributed to police officers becoming less competent and capable when it comes to effectively communicating in a confrontational situation. If you have handcuffs, a baton and spray, then it is unlikely that you would try to arrest a suspect and then struggle on the floor when you have the means to bring the situation under control a lot more quickly and safely and with less effort. However, officers can be too quick to resort to using equipment than spending time looking for a less forceful solution. All officers are trained and fully aware of their responsibilities in terms of using force and they would far sooner make an arrest where the suspect is fully compliant than one where they have to use restraining measures. The equipment is there to protect the officers in worst-case scenarios to ensure that any arrest is conducted with the minimum use of force required in correlation to the threat faced; but it is not designed to be the first option, and it is far more desirable that an officer works hard to communicate effectively. Indeed, the key part of any police officer's duty is their communication skills, especially when trying to establish calm and control in confrontational situations. The most competent police officers are the ones with excellent ability to converse with a wide variety of people and adapt their approach to the situation and persons they are facing. However, it has always been extremely difficult to talk someone into being arrested when they clearly do not want to comply or accompany you to the station, so this is no argument against protective equipment. I just think it is important to point out that police officers' general ability to communicate in tense situations has declined slightly over the years and this may be partly due to the introduction of these additional control measures and tactics.

Yet another difficulty that modern officers now face is that everyone has a mobile phone. Whilst mobiles are great in some ways and generally improve lines of communication, they can be hugely problematic when it comes to people live-streaming incidents. Crowds can start to form around the incident and this can mean that confrontational situations take longer than necessary to resolve. This sort of attention places police officers under enormous pressure to resolve the incident as quickly as possible. On the whole, the quicker a situation can be calmed down and resolved, the better it is for all involved; as the longer you remain on the street trying to persuade someone to calmly step into a police van, the more at risk you are. Allowing the situation or incident to escalate beyond the control of the officers on scene puts both the officers and anyone who is in the vicinity at risk, which explains why some officers feel the need to use force to restrain and arrest someone much sooner than those in the job may have done a few years ago. Every officer must find a balance between communicating effectively when explaining the situation to those involved and bringing the confrontation to a swift conclusion, and this is hard to do with the added pressure of commentators on social media. You need to be aware that society is changing and people can now react in a very short space of time to an incident and will be made aware of it via social media.

So, back to your personal-issue equipment: having been given all these toys to play with and having a utility belt that resembles something out of a Batman film, police officers go out into the big wide world to face what society can throw at them … and sometimes that literally means thrown!

Amid all these dangers, how can officers stay safe when they're doing the *Dixon of Dock Green* walk? Despite reports or accounts to the contrary, police officers do still walk on the streets on what is called foot patrol or walking the beat. The beat used to be a smaller area of the policing borough you were posted to and then patrolled. Even today, police officers should be prepared to be sent out on foot patrol in a specific area, and, as I mentioned earlier, on many occasions this is done alone.

But how do you stay safe? Staying safe essentially comes down to using your own observation skills, awareness, experience – what is commonly known as being 'streetwise'. Policing now places a large emphasis on delivering risk assessment and health and safety training. You will be trained to identify and recognise the nature of the risk and if you are sent to a specific incident, you will be advised if there is information of any weapons or specific risk at the address. There might even be a rendez-vous point identified before going to the call. These are used when either the control room or maybe a supervising officer decides that the call poses such a risk to those attending that they need to meet up somewhere safe first and then deal with it collectively.

Risk can come in many forms, such as someone coming at you with a knife, or in less obviously threatening ways: maybe you are working near rivers, railway lines or fast moving traffic. The police service now identifies only two levels of risk: situations are either high risk or unknown risk. The default title for a call that the control room are unsure of is usually 'a disturbance', and that can cover anything from an argument over what TV show to watch to a serious assault being committed. At other times, you will be despatched to more obviously high-risk calls that sound horrendous – large groups fighting, knives being used and persons reportedly stabbed. Such a call immediately sounds high risk from the fighting and weapons being used, and possibly one where a rendezvous point will be assigned. I can only suggest that you keep an open mind for every call you deal with and that you consider the following things: remain alert and consider everything you see, everything you hear, whatever you are told and what you can smell. The key thing here is information and the more information you can gather about what you are dealing with then the better your risk assessment will be. When dealing with any call your information-gathering skills should go into overdrive as you try to establish as much detail about what sort of disturbance you are walking into.

You have to keep your wits about you and be aware of your surroundings – advice I would have welcomed before I joined. I very nearly fell foul of this myself when one night we were involved in a vehicle pursuit for over ten minutes through the streets of Tooting and then into Mitcham. Eventually the vehicle stopped with all four wheels locked and skidded to a halt, and then the driver leapt out of the car and ran away across a level crossing. It was about 2 a.m. so there was no danger of trains running on the line, so off I went chasing after my suspected car thief as he ran along the railway tracks in a scene reminiscent of so many TV shows. Being thirty years younger than I am now and having eaten considerably fewer takeaway meals, I managed to catch the suspect within fifty metres and walked him back to the level crossing and my waiting colleagues. As we reached them, I was feeling pretty proud of myself and stopped in front of my driver Mick 'Dutchie' Holland (if you need to ask about his nickname you may be considering the wrong job!), who was calmly waiting for me to return with said suspect.

His reaction quite literally could have knocked me down with a feather. He pushed me very forcefully with both hands, causing me and my suspect to stagger back and almost fall over. As I was doing my best goldfish impersonation, he very calmly and with that knowing, smug smile that all old-school cops had at the time, pointed to the floor. I looked down and noticed he was pointing at the live rail and I must have almost stepped on top of it with my suspect. 'Just because the bloody trains have stopped running, doesn't mean the electricity has!' He then just as calmly turned and walked back to our car and said, 'Come on then before you electrocute yourself and the poor bugger in the process.' It was a very sobering lesson for me as a young and keen PC, but also a very valuable one and one I used throughout my career. My advice would be you must be aware of your surroundings at all times and remember to keep on doing those risk assessments.

It's not just danger on the streets you need to be aware of: even your fellow officers may well pose their own risks to your well-being and safety. There is a history of practical jokes and gags being played throughout the police service and you should expect some form of what may be called 'humour' to be directed at you at some point. During one night duty at Mitcham I was driving the area car Victor Five with my radio operator, a police constable nicknamed 'Mad Jack' and a special constable called Barry. Jack's nickname was very apt as he was as mad as a box of frogs. On this particular night, Barry had decided to bring in to work a couple of thunder flashes which, I found out later, Jack had asked him to do. To this day I have no idea what Jack intended using these for, but Barry, being keen and willing to oblige, brought them in from his Territorial Army equipment. The two giggling conspirators eventually confessed their ill-conceived plan half way through the night, when one of the thunder flashes rolled under my seat and lodged near the brake pedal. I screeched the car to a halt somewhere in Mitcham at about 1.30 a.m. and shouted, 'What the f*** is that and what the f*** is it doing in my car?' After a half-arsed explanation and some arm-twisting from me, I managed to persuade them that their initial plan of lighting and throwing it under the station sergeant's desk whilst he was sitting there was not the best idea! Sergeant Joe was only over at Mitcham to cover for our own sergeant's being off for the night, and greeting him with a thunder flash under his rear end would not go down well.

We finally settled on lighting it in the station yard and placing it on a window ledge outside the office where the rest of our team were sitting having their mid-shift refreshments. Our choice of refreshment in the late '80s was very limited and the only places open after 1 a.m. were a kebab shop or the all-night bakers on Croydon Road to pick up a hot pasty or sausage roll. Most of the shift used to eat together around 2 a.m. when the calls tended to slow up and things quietened down. We knew most of our team would be gathered together in the downstairs office over cups of tea, pasties and sausage rolls. How Jack contained his giggling as he crept up and placed this thing I have no idea, but once he lit it the thing went off like a rocket, fizzing and buzzing so loudly I was sure we would wake up the whole neighbourhood. The boys in the office heard the commotion and realised we were missing and clearly up to no good. Sitting nearest the open window was Andy, who was half way through his Cornish pasty. Andy was never usually that quick to move but he excelled himself that night and leapt up to slam the window shut. As his hands reached the window, the thunder flash went off and the glass disintegrated over his outstretched hand. As we ran inside the building, I could hear Sergeant Joe shouting, 'What the f***ing hell was that, are we under attack?' The building had rocked under the detonation and Andy was running round the office with blood pouring from his hand.

The three of us sheepishly peered round the corner to the scene of uproar and carnage as kebabs and pasties etc. had been thrown across the floor. First aid was rendered to Andy after he was first politely told to 'Stand the f*** still you tosser, you are bleeding all over the pasties!' Even in the midst of chaos there are still some priorities to observe and the team grub was sacrosanct. I dutifully offered to rush Andy to the nearest A & E to get his hand stitched whilst Jack borrowed Andy's patrol car and replenished the stock of pasties that had been contaminated by blood after Andy danced round the room spraying blood everywhere. The team were reluctant to consume the remaining pasties and sausage rolls due to a few specks of blood but you couldn't blame them, as Andy was originally from Molesey and they might be contagious.

The station occurrence book was filled in and noted the damage to the window with a sort-of accurate report. The entry read: 'a large gust of wind blew the office window open as PC Andy ****** was reaching up to shut it, causing window to smash and cut the officer's hand causing injury as reported. Officer was not placed sick and window to be repaired on day duty.'

The resulting references to *The Italian Job* – 'You were only supposed to blow the bloody window shut' – continued for a few months. Barry never darkened the inside of my vehicle again and, to this day, Andy has a nice crescent-shaped scar on his hand. Clearly, the dangers of police work are not all outside the station.

So, how do you approach risky or dangerous situations and what type of instruction and training do you receive? We have already discovered there are two levels of risk, high and unknown. Current police training identifies three areas where risk may come from and there is a helpful memory aide to remember them. It is called 'POP' which stands for 'person, object, place' and it entails the need for every police officer to consider what risks or threats may be posed by the person(s), the place itself and any objects either carried by the person(s) or simply present at the scene. Take a straight-forward call to a person shouting and swearing in the street; in this case, the risk comes from the person. A call to a disturbance where some-one is in possession of a knife is a situation wherein the object becomes the source of the risk. Lastly, if you are dealing with someone in the kitchen of a private house with lots of knives around or maybe alongside a river, it is the place that becomes the greatest risk.

To deal with these three elements there is another mnemonic. The police training manual really likes them and there are literally hundreds of them for all sorts of things. To deal with risks or threat posed by our 'POP' then we would apply the principle of 'RARA'; don't worry, you have not ventured off into some kind of police-y Harry Potter world!

RARA helps you remember that there are four ways of dealing with any risk: remove the risk, avoid the risk, reduce the risk and, lastly, accept the risk. For any incident you deal with, however risky or dangerous, you should apply these four tactics. You would ask yourself, 'Can I remove the risk?' i.e. either by speaking to the house occupants in a different room or removing any sharp objects from the surroundings. You could 'avoid' the risk by asking the people involved to stay away from the source of the risk. Reducing the risk could involve placing yourself between the person and any object you are concerned about, so reducing the possibility they will pick it up and use it. Finally, sometimes you just have to accept the risk and get on with dealing with the incident. It may look strange if you start tidying up knives and there are probably other sharp objects all around the room. Remember forewarned is forearmed. Identifying danger is all part of the information gathering process that will become second nature to you as a police officer.

So, now you know what equipment you have to protect yourself with and how to conduct accurate risk assessments, how dangerous can working as a police officer really be?

The clearest answer to the question is that policing can be a dangerous occupation. Although you are given defensive equipment and training, you are always potentially dealing with aggressive situations and violent people. The danger changes on a daily basis. Uniformed officers on response teams who are part of the so-called front line will face potentially dangerous situations almost every day. An investigative detective on a counter-terrorist or a cyber-crime unit, on the other hand, is rarely confronted by hostile situations or individuals as their role is predominantly investigative. Policing is a wide-ranging and varied occupation with many specialisms available to you once you have completed your probationary period. The normal probationary period is currently two years long for the majority of officers joining, although there are direct-entry schemes for superintendents and inspectors. Once you have completed your probation, the choice is largely yours when it comes to deciding how you want to develop your policing career.

You are also given training in how to effectively communicate and take control of challenging situations and you will learn all about the numerous laws and offences that may apply. That sounds a lot of training and knowledge for one person, so it's no surprise that one of the most frequently asked questions on any initial police training course is, 'What do I need to know and do I need to know all of it?'

So, what exactly do you need to learn to be a police officer and how long will it all take?

CHAPTER 3

WHAT DO YOU NEED

TO KNOW?

Counting everything you need to know to be a police officer is like measuring the proverbial piece of string, as you could spend your entire career studying laws, policies, guidelines and codes of practice. Policing has to be one of the most regulated professions in the UK. There are laws that must be followed, policies that must be adhered to, guidance notes and discipline rules that you must also comply with. The sheer volume of material is often enough to put most people off from starting or completing the initial training, so let's make this as easy as possible. My favourite analogy is the age-old comedy question, 'How do you eat an elephant?' And the answer is, 'One bite at a time.' Our first 'bite' concerns what you need to do before you join and, currently, you need to obtain a Certificate in Knowledge of Policing (CKP). When this qualification was introduced a few years ago, the policy changed so that prospective applicants for almost every police force were required to obtain this qualification before they can be considered for a position as a police officer. Plans are currently being developed by the College of Policing to replace the CKP with the Policing Educational Qualification Framework (PEQF), which will provide both an apprenticeship scheme as part of the application for new recruits, and qualifications that recognise the knowledge and experience of officers at all ranks. We could spend an entire book looking at the history of policing and how Scottish forces are separate to England and Wales and so on, but for simplicity's sake, if you are thinking of joining then check with your preferred force if they require a CKP. There are also some direct entry schemes for graduates and at some senior levels, but for most you will need a CKP before you will be offered a date to join.

The CKP is a theory-based qualification similar to a National Vocational Qualification (NVQ) and the course content is controlled by the College of Policing. The training is offered by various private companies that are all licensed by the College of Policing and the course costs around £800–900 for each individual, and is self-funded. Some forces, including the Metropolitan Police, offer their own internal CKP course which is completed prior to officially joining, but again, you have to fund this qualification yourself. The biggest point of controversy here is the cost of the qualification and the fact it does not always guarantee you employment as a police officer. Not everyone can afford to spend £900 on an educational qualification and, although there are loans available from some forces, the cost of the scheme has its critics.

The CKP can be completed by attending daily or weekly classroom lectures or by distance learning via an online system, depending on which course provider you select. It covers the laws, legislation, policies and guidelines applicable to all police officers and essentially provides the theory side of policing. You will learn about risk assessments, memory aides and incidents such as theft, assault and criminal damage, along with many other offences that you may encounter as an operational officer in your first few years. It only covers the more common offences that you will deal with, so the more serious or complex issues such as fraud or murder are not taught in any great depth. Do not picture yourself in your first couple of years as the lead investigator for a murder and solving the crime as you've seen on TV. This is real life and that sort of training takes longer.

Whilst this all might sound fairly straight-forward, do not underestimate the volume of knowledge needed to pass the CKP as the quantity of reading and studying involved has surprised many, including those who already have a degree. But it is worth sticking with, as once you have passed the CKP, the fun begins as you try to apply the theory of policing to your actual training. As part of the initial training you will have to complete assessed role plays, for which you play the part of a police officer and you are given a scenario to deal with whilst being assessed by an instructor. The scenario could be something like reporting a car that's been damaged or maybe something has been stolen. The key here is for you to ask the right sort of questions as you investigate the allegation and then report the crime. The other role player will answer your questions, provided you ask the right ones at the right time, but they may not supply you with all the information you need so it is very important that you are able to quickly identify the nature of the crime. For example, to verify a report of criminal damage there must be property that's been damaged or destroyed either intentionally or recklessly and without lawful excuse. The questions you ask in the role play will establish these points to prove as you identify the offence by using the definitions you have learnt.

There will also be arrest and stop and search scenarios, which involve you being assessed whilst you stop someone and give the correct legal grounds required to justify searching them and possibly arresting them. Once again, you need to know how to define the nature of the offence; so for example, you must know the legal definition of an offensive weapon. A successful stop and search is not necessarily simply down to finding the actual object but more about how the grounds for the search are given and explained and then how the search is conducted. Each and every time you conduct a search of a person, follow the steps of the mnemonic, 'Gowisely', which you will learn about during your training. Essentially, it covers your grounds, what you are searching for, who you are and the person's entitlement to a copy of the search record, and this information must be given prior to every search.

I was role playing one day for the initial training and the recruit started searching me after giving an excellent explanation of their grounds, the object they were looking for and my entitlement etc. I had hidden a small knife and the officer knew I had been seen with a knife, and she was now searching for it. She conducted a very thorough and professional search but failed to find the knife hidden in a very small pocket on the sleeve of my fleece. The main reason she missed finding it was because I started talking to deliberately distract her from the search. She still passed the role play as her introduction, explanation of her grounds and searching method were very good, but she had allowed herself to be distracted by the suspect and therefore missed the pocket with the knife. There is a great deal to learn and the instructors will not expect you to know everything straight away. Once you have learnt the theory side of things, the real part of understanding how to be a police officer comes, like everything else, with practice.

Studying hard to learn a lot of laws and policies and then applying these during some play acting in a classroom sounds pretty easy, but there is so much more to police training. The one thing that arguably separates the good police officers from the average ones is their ability to communicate. One of my pet hates is walking past a police car or seeing officers on the streets with their heads down staring intently at a mobile phone. I know that modern life is reliant on technology but whilst policing, your ability to communicate is possibly your best tool. Eye contact and saying 'Hello' or 'Good morning/ afternoon' can often defuse a situation or simply ingratiate you to the people you meet whilst you're on duty. If you are considering policing as a career, then work on your social skills as, in my opinion, being able to converse with people seems to be a vanishing characteristic. After all, police officers cannot interview people via text message, e-mail or WhatsApp.

The other issue about relying on technology is that it has led officers to fall foul of discipline regulations and some have even committed offences when using their smartphones and laptops. There have been several high-profile cases where officers have unlawfully sent images or text messages about a case. If the discipline unit receive an allegation of wrongdoing by a police officer, then they have the same powers as any police officer has in any investigation to seize and examine the evidence. This can include personal computers and mobile phones which will then be fully examined and analysed for every message and image sent or received. During our CKP courses, at the start of the stop and search lecture I run through a small exercise where I get the class to hand their mobile phone to another person. There are several looks of anxiety and sometimes horror when I tell them their phone will now be examined and their colleagues can open up any message and view any image on their phone.

There is also the issue of personal security when it comes to social media accounts. Before you are accepted as a police officer, you will go through a vetting process which includes background checks into your own life as well as your friends and family. You will be advised as to how to make your presence online and on social media more secure. Ask yourself this: do you actually know everyone you are friends with on Facebook or follow on Twitter? Have you met them? How much information do they know about you? What information is out there about you on the World Wide Web?

I don't want to make you paranoid about this, but always consider these things before you tweet or post a comment on Facebook. Is it something you would be happy for your parents to read? Would you say it to someone's face? If the answer is no to either of these questions, don't post it, not even to your close friends. Once you have sent it, you have no control over what the recipient does with it or if anyone else will get to see it. There is a code of conduct for police officers as society expects the best from their police service. So, before joining or even applying for the police, have a look at your Instagram, Facebook and Twitter accounts and maybe have a bit of a spring clean through your contacts and comments. Once that is done, always keep the 'parent' question in your head and never ever be tempted to use any form of social media when drunk!

Having sorted out your online presence, what sort of shape do you need to be in physically to be in the police? Is there a height and weight restriction and how fit do you need to be?

There is no longer a height restriction for police officers. When I joined in 1979, men had to be at least 5ft 8in. and women 5ft 4in. without high heels ... for the women, that is! I have to say, looking at some of my former colleagues I wonder if they did not borrow their mums' shoes for the assessment day to reach 5ft 8in. ... no names, Paulo! I have seen and heard of all sorts of techniques practised by some trying to join who were just under the height limit; and I have to admit, I am hardly considered lofty standing just 5ft 11in. in my socks! Padded socks, heel lifts in their socks and all sorts of minor adjustments were done to try and stretch to that magical 5ft 8in. and 5ft 4in. Luckily that is now all in the past, although it still makes me smile when I think back to how we used to deliberately put a very tall officer out on foot patrol with one who was not quite so tall! One of my former sergeants was 6ft 7in. tall and it always made me laugh when I heard people say, 'Ooh, you're tall aren't you?' as if it was a surprise to him! If only I had a pound for every time he heard that question, I would be writing this from my yacht in the Caribbean. We became used to this opening exchange with everyone we met whilst working together at Mitcham and his stock answer became, 'I'm 5ft 19in. tall', which was usually met with confused silence and then rapid counting with their fingers. Basic maths is also a requirement for police officers, so if you have now resorted to taking your shoes and socks off to work out his height, you may be considering the wrong career. So, it doesn't matter how short or tall you are these days to apply to become a police officer. Size really doesn't matter for policing, although there may be some roles and tasks that would be a challenge. Being 6ft 7in. tall may be a challenge when riding a horse or sitting in a small police patrol car, similar to the mini metro as we used to have. Watching Cliff climb in and out of our panda cars was always entertaining – even more so when we put him in the back of the two-door car! We could have removed the front seat and he still could have driven the thing from the back seat with his long legs.

That's height covered, but what about the tricky subject of weight? All prospective police officers have to undergo a medical assessment and answer a medical questionnaire, as the police service needs to be sure you are physically fit for the job. They will test your blood pressure, test your eyesight and hearing and measure your height and weight. After calculating that dreaded Body Mass Index (BMI), you will be subjected to the annual fitness examination. Every police recruit must meet the required level in the bleep test, which is level 5.4 and described by most as little more than a light jog. If you ask most serving officers, they will happily tell you that the bleep test is easy and just a jog up and down the room. I have a family member who has recently applied to join the police, and so I offered to help her with the bleep test. I was thrilled that I managed to reach level 5.4 with some comfort but it was starting to get difficult and my training partner found it tough going the first time. After a few more attempts and practising breathing right and turning at the right pace she mastered it and was successful at her assessment day.

I would suggest that anyone applying to join should practise the bleep test first and ignore the 'it's easy' brigade. If you play regular sport – and I mean active sport, not chess or snooker, with no disrespect to either, but something that requires physical exertion – then you should have no problem. But is it easy? Well, not exactly and like most things it is only easy if you have done it a few times before and there is a routine or technique to be acquired. There is always a warm-up before the bleep test. The test involves jogging between two fixed points about 15 metres apart. The machine bleeps at the moment you are required to reach the point you are running towards. As the test progresses, the bleep frequency increases so you must run faster to keep up in time with the bleep. You can receive two warnings if you are too slow on your turns before they fail you. Hopefully, you will pass first time, but occasionally some applicants fail their first attempt and are usually given another chance on a different date. This gives them a chance to practise and prepare for the test, as running in time to a series of bleeps that gradually increase in regularity is not easy to achieve if it is your first attempt.

Being overweight can be an issue, but the real test is the fitness assessment which is given to every recruit on their assessment days and then repeated during basic officer safety training in your initial training. You will see some officers and think 'How on earth have they passed a fitness test?', and obviously there are some exceptions to the rule as the police are an equal opportunities employer and subject to employment law. Whilst all officers are subject to a rigorous medical examination, not every single police officer is able to complete the bleep test. I know of one detective who lost a leg through illness a few years ago. He is still serving and passed as fit for his investigative role, and he did not have to do the bleep test. As a general rule, however, every applicant must pass the fitness test and be considered medically able for the job.

Having ensured you are medically suitable and physically fit enough for a policing career, what next?

You will be vetted, and that requires you to fill in a form and supply some proof of identity, like a passport or a birth certificate. You will also have to list your parents' names and dates of birth, details of any siblings and your partner's name, date of birth and occupation. These are all checked to ensure there are no reasons why you should not become a police officer. Significant security issues could potentially be caused if you lived with or were related to someone who was actively involved in crime. That does not automatically mean you would be prevented from joining but, as in many other instances, each case would be decided according to its own circumstances. There is no definitive 'My brother has been convicted of a serious assault so does that stop me joining?' scenario. It would depend on many factors, including the offence itself and the closeness of the relationship with whoever was involved. The final decision has much to do with openness and transparency, so that the police can make an informed decision when it comes to the person's employment.

The actual vetting process can take a long time depending on which force you are applying for and how many people they are looking to recruit at that time. The rules and regulations have changed a lot since I first joined. We used to be required to submit a form asking for permission to co-habit with your partner or to get married and you had to provide your prospective spouse's name, and all applications had to be checked and approved. Two divorces down the line and I somehow wish they had taken a bit longer to consider my marriages! That brings me to another aspect you had to report: separating from your spouse and starting divorce proceedings. Separations had to be alerted to the police service and then they were officially 'approved', although I am not sure how they would have refused you permission to divorce. Beyond these applications, the job itself had a reputation as not being con-ducive to long and happy marriages.

I know of one former colleague who was actually refused permission by his chief superintendent to marry his second wife. Apparently background checks had revealed that one of her close relations had been a member of the Irish Republican Army and this was in the 1980s when the terror threat was high from the IRA. This little hiccup in the nuptials was only resolved when the chief superintendent was informed that her relative was actually deceased and had been so for twenty years. Rank and seniority is not a barrier to stupid and ill-informed decisions, even in the police service.

Buying a house was also a bureaucratic affair, as you had to ask for permission to live at a certain address beforehand. This was so that the address and your prospective neighbours could be checked for any criminal activity to see whether it was a 'suitable' address for a police officer. A good friend and former colleague of mine faced this problem after the check discovered that his next-door neighbour-to-be had a conviction for armed robbery. This caused a slight problem as my colleague had already started the purchase negotiations, thinking it wouldn't be a problem. His chief superintendent declined his application to buy the flat. My friend then went to the local police station collator's office, which is where all records of local criminals were kept in the late '80s, and checked his prospective neighbour's criminal history. It turned out the armed robbery conviction was from the 1950s and the criminal in question was now in his seventies and moving around on a Zimmer frame. Needless to say, my friend queried the decision and it was reversed by the chief superintendent and permission was given for the flat purchase. He went on to live next to this septuagenarian criminal who caused problems on a weekly basis by asking my colleague to put his bins out for him.

In most circumstances the report would be returned to you with 'approved' stamped on it and you could then proceed with your house purchase. In the Metropolitan Police, there was also a regulation that you had to live within twenty-five miles of Charing Cross. This regulation dated from the 1800s and was created to ensure that all officers could attend a place of duty in the Metropolitan Police area if required to do so.

To prove your address fit the criteria, you had to go into the administration office at the police station where they had a large map of London. There was a pin stuck directly on top of Charing Cross with a length of thread attached to it and a second pin. The thread counted for twenty-five miles and so you took it and located the second pin where you intended to buy a property. If the pin reached without breaking the thread then you could apply to buy your house! In some offices the cotton thread must have been replaced by an elastic band, considering the addresses of some of the applications.

I am pleased to tell you that the modern police service has removed some parts of this bureaucracy, although they will still need to be informed of marriages etc. You no longer have to drag a piece of thread across a wall-mounted map, but some forces still insist that officers live within their force area. This is a contentious point, as many good candidates are being prevented from applying for their chosen force due to where their registered address happens to be. Parents may have moved and so the family home is now outside the area the individual grew up in. Maybe they have been off to university or have been travelling the world and are now renting or temporarily staying with family or friends but wish to return to the area they know well. It seems a very blinkered view for forces to only recruit so-called 'local' applicants. The idea is that local applicants know the area well enough to police it and so are 'representative' of the community they are policing. As is typical of many policies in policing, this one has not been properly thought through and the broad-brush approach does not take account of diverse personal circumstances – quite the opposite to the approach of your initial training, which instructs you to deal with each case based on its own particular circumstances. If this applies to you and you find yourself being initially refused permission to join because of a residential condition, then appeal the decision and explain your points clearly and concisely. In many instances, these decisions are made by someone who is just adhering strictly to the policy and quite often they are not police officers. Do not take the first refusal as a definitive answer and explain the qualities you will bring to the role and how you will benefit that local community.

At some point – and it is up to you when and how you mention it – you will need to tell your family you are joining the police. Only you know what sort of reaction you will face and what they will think, but the big question for you is, 'Will it change the way they see me and will it change me as a person?'

CHAPTER 4

WHAT WILL MY FRIENDS

AND FAMILY THINK?

Do you think your life will change when you become a police officer? It is highly likely the job will change your outlook, your loyalties, your friendships, your personality and your characteristics in many ways. That fact may take a while to sink in, but you really will change. You may have to re-assess some friendships and relationships and decide if any of them will cause you a problem as a serving police officer. Are there some people you know who are committing illegal acts or maybe just sailing a bit too close to the wind in terms of their activities? I am really talking about the more serious criminal

activities here and not just motoring offences. I am not advocating disinheriting or distancing yourselves from mum or dad
because they drive too quickly or park on double yellow lines!
Friends who become a bit lively on a Saturday night after a few
drinks aren't a problem, but the shouty or sweary types that
inevitably attract the attention of patrolling officers may be the
ones you need to consider avoiding. You must also consider those
you know who take illegal substances. You need to ask yourself
this question: could my relationship with this person bring me
into conflict in my role as a police officer?

Understandably, as a police officer you will become more
aware of what is legal and, more importantly, what is illegal
and the implications of indulging in any illegal activities. One
misconception is that police officers cannot have any convictions
at all to work or remain working as a police officer. Motoring
offences, such as speeding or using a mobile phone when
driving, committed by serving officers must be reported to
their supervisors. This applies whether the offence is committed
on or off duty, and it is a discipline offence if you fail to do
so. You are also required to report any civil court proceedings
for non-payment of fines, any debt and legal or civil disputes
that you may become involved in. Essentially, any time you are
involved in a court appearance or hearing it has to be reported
to your supervisors whilst you are a serving police officer. It
does not automatically mean officers will be dismissed from the

police service, although obviously there is a greater issue if you commit any offences whilst on duty. Some of the minor criminal offences are treated similarly to traffic infringements, but it does depend on the circumstances of each case. In the main, criminal convictions usually mean dismissal from the police service or being required to resign, which effectively means the same thing. Traffic offences are not viewed as critically, but it does depend on the case and clearly causing death by dangerous driving may understandably result in dismissal from the police service. It will largely depend on the public impact of the incident itself, the seriousness of the charge and if you are convicted in court.

Public confidence in the police service is essential as we police by public consent – a phrase you will hear often in your training and during your policing career. You need to remember that police officers are subject to a fairly strict discipline code and, although you may be acquitted at court, you may still have to answer a case involving a breach of the discipline code. Effectively, the police service has two bites at the cherry when it comes to an officer's career if an offence has been committed. First you have to wait and see if you are convicted at court and, if not, then you must look into whether you have breached the discipline code; and both can result in an officer's dismissal from the police. It is likely that if you are convicted of a criminal offence, you will have undoubtedly breached the discipline code and may be dismissed from the service.

This does not mean police officers live like saints or have some kind of monastic lifestyle, but they are aware of the need to be law abiding. Their role is hard and very demanding, and there has to be an outlet of this pressure on occasion. The old adage 'work hard, play hard' was very true of my time in the police and nothing much has changed. The key here is to understand what you can and cannot do and knowing when to stop, which is often difficult when alcohol or other influences, such as peer pressure, are involved. I could happily fill this book with tales of raucous nights out that were pretty rock and roll (but without the drugs!). Times have changed now, however, and there is a much greater focus on monitoring or observing officers' conduct. Restraint is extremely important for modern police officers due to a number of factors and changes in society. The proliferation of CCTV and camera phones, together with the easy access to social media, means that any misbehaviour can be instantly captured for all eternity. The increase in online news outlets and constant news updates raise the possibility of poor behaviour being highlighted now much more than it ever used to be. Monitoring groups and police watchdogs independently observe and report any misdemeanour committed by officers. An image or video posted on social media can be viewed by thousands before the officer or the police themselves have an opportunity to respond or explain the circumstances. Modern officers need to be far more aware and conscious of their actions and words being observed and recorded than officers from my era ever had to be.

Whilst having to obtain permission to marry and divorce may have stopped, it is important to understand that policing is not a regular occupation and it is an exceptionally demanding job. It will place stress and strain on any relationship as, inevitably, there will be some parts of your work that will stay with you when you get home. The support by partners of serving officers cannot be underestimated and, in many ways, they have the more difficult role. They will frequently not understand what is happening at work and will have no way of knowing why you are acting differently when you get home. Good communication skills are required just as much when you get home as whilst you are at work.

Policing really is like no other occupation, aside from maybe the armed forces, in terms of the way it requires you either to work with little or no notice or even cancel your leave or days off. The Metropolitan Police show a great video at passing-out parades and during their recruit training which depicts a scene where you miss your partner's birthday because of work, and they swiftly become an ex-partner…

The wonderful phrase 'exigency of duty', used by so many senior officers when they require you to work at short notice, has never been completely explained to those it affects. It essentially means that at any time, a senior officer can decide that an incident or criminal activity is an 'exigency' and additional police officers are required to deal with it. The definition in the *Oxford English Dictionary* of 'exigency' is 'an urgent need or demand', so you can see how it can have a wide meaning when you apply it to policing. The senior officer for your policing area may decide that any problem they face meets this 'urgent need or demand' criteria and tell officers on leave or at the end of their shift that they are now required to be on duty until such need has been dealt with. Most experienced officers will tell you this is why they hardly ever answer a phone call from a withheld number when they are off duty, unless they want to earn overtime. Most police phone numbers come up as withheld when you dial out from a police station, hence the practice of letting any calls from such numbers go to your answerphone. In truth, leaving the call unanswered may only delay the inevitable, as you would have some difficult questions to answer if a message was left for you to 'urgently report yourself on duty as soon as possible' and you failed to do so.

In 1985, just after the disorder at Broadwater Farm in Tottenham and the brutal murder of PC Keith Blakelock, the Met Police initiated twelve-hour tours for all officers and kept a substantial reserve contingent available on duty. In effect, this meant that the night-duty team came in to work for 6 p.m.

but were held on standby at their police stations and did not take over from the late turn until 10 p.m. The late turn team then went on standby from 10 p.m. until 2 a.m. and then went home. The early turn worked from 6 a.m. until 2 p.m. and then went on standby until 6 p.m., and so this meant that from 2 p.m. until 2 a.m. the Met had a ready available contingent of extra resources. In the 2011 riots, the Met went one step further by making the whole force work a twelve-hour shift, which meant two shifts working to cover the 24-hour period and one whole shift being on standby. This was achieved by making the early turn work from 6 a.m. until 6 p.m. and then the night duty team work from 6 p.m. until 6 a.m., and the team scheduled to be late turn, 2–10 p.m., were available for deployment anywhere in the force area. This was replicated across some other police forces in the UK as the disorder spread, and there were significant additional police resources deployed across the UK. London had officers from all the home county forces working in the capital and also from as far afield as Wales and Scotland. During times of exceptional demand on the police service, such as any serious disorder or terror attack, then you may well be called in for extended hours of duty and this inevitably places a strain on you and your family life.

There may be some point in any policing career where you will be kept on duty or even called in to work during your time off and you will have to miss a family function.

When I eventually retired after thirty years, I had to almost re-introduce myself to some of my family members as I hadn't seen them for about twenty years. I had to be introduced to some of my cousins' children as I had never met them and to them I had almost turned into this fictional character! I had become 'Graham the Policeman' whom they had all heard about but had never seen. As an only child, I did feel guilty working on Christmas Day and not being with my mum, although she had a wide circle of friends and family that she used to visit. Christmas had never really been a fun-filled family affair in my house growing up, as Dad had left when I was eight years old. We seemed to spend the following few years staying with relatives, which I always resented as I just wanted to be home and near my own friends. I never actually spent another Christmas Day with my dad, and it is possible that my childhood memories of less-than-happy Christmases meant I was content to work instead. I worked at least twenty Christmas Days and more than twenty New Year's Eves during my policing service, with my record being the time I worked sixteen hours as a custody officer at Hammersmith police station one Christmas Day, clocking in at 6 a.m. and clocking out at 10 p.m. There had been no other volunteers to be the custody officer for the late turn shift on Christmas Day, yet several others fancied the double-time payment for the early shift. Early turn on Christmas Day also meant being home by

3 p.m. for dinner and presents. The local duties sergeant, realising what was happening, posted me with my own team as early turn initially and left the late turn blank and asked again for volunteers. I was the only applicant and so he duly allocated me the late turn as well. This initiated all sorts of moans and groans from some disgruntled colleagues, but not surprisingly, when he and I both offered to relinquish my late turn shift to those complaining, they withdrew their applications; and so I spent sixteen hours on a Christmas Day as the custody officer. My anticipated 10 p.m. finish was then lengthened when the last prisoner of the day turned out to be a drunk driver and I eventually walked out just after midnight after a very long and festive tour of duty. Suffice to say I was not overly full of the season's greetings for the next few days, although the eighteen hours at double-time in my pay packet the following month did raise a smile.

It is largely up to you to organise your working life and book off Christmas or New Year or any other significant date. I know some officers in London who somehow have never worked a New Year's Eve or Notting Hill Carnival, even though both occasions are allegedly compulsory working days for the whole of the Metropolitan Police, including the commissioner. Once the number of officers required for the events has been decided, the remaining officers can apply to have the days off. You can sometimes apply to take both those days off if it is amongst a period of your holiday leave, so you would book off 24 December until 4 January inclusive. There is a limit, though, to how many officers can book extended periods of leave over both the Carnival and New Year, and there is usually a waiting list. This applies to similar events elsewhere in the UK, for example, officers in Scotland have to be available for the significant policing operation for Hogmanay in Edinburgh.

So you need to be aware that at some point, unless you are very well organised and more than a little bit fortunate, you will work a Christmas Day and some bank holidays. It may also come as a surprise to some that you will also be expected to work on your birthday! On one of my most recent CKP courses, one student seemed shocked when it was explained to her that she would not be automatically allowed to have her birthday as a leave day. It was explained that policing is a 24/7 occupation, and to some extent bank holidays and Christmas are treated as normal working days, so why on earth would the police service make an allowance for individual officers' birthdays?

At some point, hopefully, you will have discussed your plans to join the police service with your family, friends and partner. I know of a few recruits who have actually started training and even reached their passing-out parade before telling their family that they have joined the police service. I worked with a great lad from Northern Ireland in the late '80s who kept it a very closely guarded secret that he was a Metropolitan Police officer. He used to return home to Belfast very occasionally and visit his parents under the cover of darkness due to the Troubles over there. They knew what he actually did in London but his extended family and friends in Northern Ireland thought he worked in an office in the capital. Remember, back then there were no mobile phones, no internet and no social media, so it was slightly easier to keep your work and private life hidden. Police officers were a clear target for the Provisional IRA at that time, so my colleague was very careful when making any visits home and, on every occasion, he had to make a written request for permission to the Metropolitan Police. He had to hand in his warrant card to the Metropolitan Police Special Branch so that he had nothing identifying him as a police officer whilst he was in Northern Ireland. I visited Northern Ireland myself with the Metropolitan Police football club in the early '90s to play in a national police cup competition against the Royal Ulster Constabulary in Northern Ireland. I remember the whole touring party, which was made up entirely of serving officers, being met at Heathrow airport by a special branch officer who took the warrant cards off every person. We got them back when we landed back at Heathrow a couple of days later. Throughout our stay we were escorted by Royal Ulster Constabulary (RUC) officers and we received a specific threat assessment and briefing from Special Branch and the local RUC officers about our trip, and the do's and don'ts whilst there.

Hopefully, you will be one of the many who join the police service with family and friends who are fully supportive and keen to see you succeed – and, more importantly, safe. These days, it is far easier to stay in touch and update family and friends on your well-being than when I first joined. I can remember coming back from working at Brixton during the disorder in 1981 and walking into the police section house at some unearthly hour to find several worried messages left by my mother asking me to phone home. As if that wasn't enough, the section house warden grabbed hold of me as I attempted to climb the stairs and ordered me to ring my mum. When I tried to explain that it was now close to 5 a.m. and I was sure she would be asleep, he explained she had phoned several times during the night enquiring after my welfare and, being a mum, would definitely be awake until she heard from me. Being too tired to argue, I made like *ET* and duly phoned home, and was surprised when the phone was picked up after barely one ring. Using single syllables, I explained I was off to my bed as I was back on duty in less than eight hours and, yes, I did have a clean shirt and underpants with me. Helpful hint: always let your mum know you are safe whenever there is any reported incident involving a police officer within twenty-five miles or so of where you work. It doesn't matter if you are miles away or not working with that particular unit at the time, mums, dads and families will worry about you until they hear that you are OK and the incident did not involve you. You will also develop a method of not-quite telling parents (and especially mums) what you actually do at work as a police officer. Some things are best left unsaid to your mum.

It is important that you reassure family, friends and partner of your safety, especially if they have no concept of what policing entails. They will be rightfully proud of your career, but it is understandable that they will have concerns about your safety. There have been some tragic incidents over the last few years and sadly far too many police officers have lost their lives doing the job they love. These are usually widely reported in the media and will increase any worry your loved ones have if you are working as a police officer or considering a career in policing. I talk about the training you receive and the dangers you may face elsewhere in this book, but always remember that your family and loved ones do not have that same knowledge. Your choice of career may face criticism or opposition from those closest to you due to the inherent dangers in policing. Respect their views, but also assure them of the high degree of training you receive and the support available to you as a police officer.

I would advocate discussing your policing career with those closest to you and talking through the implications your chosen career will have on those relationships. Policing is not a part-time occupation. You may have social or sporting commitments already in place and I would always encourage any prospective police officers to maintain these whenever possible. It follows the 'Peelian principles', which state that the police is the community and the community is the police, for serving officers to socialise and partake in sporting activities within their communities. As I have already explained, there may well be many demands on your time as a police officer, with weekend working, late shifts and night shifts, which can limit your involvement in activities outside the police service. Just as with managing your days off on special events, it is largely incumbent on you as an individual to maintain your commitment to friends and events.

My friends and family were completely supportive when I first joined and understood that there would be times I'd have to work instead of attending an event. In all honesty, I could have probably made more effort to take days off and attend more family functions over the years, but I was enjoying my job too much and occasionally it was convenient to be unable to attend a family event! In hindsight, I wish I had taken the days off and attended more family get-togethers, as I can now see how important they are. What I have learnt is that if your relationships with your family and friends are strong enough, then they will survive the demands of a policing career. These days, it is far easier to stay in touch with smartphones and e-mail and, over the last few years, I have even reconnected with old school friends and colleagues from my early policing career and even some family members.

Regardless of whether you have already joined or if you are considering a policing career, talk to those closest to you. You will need their help and support during your entire career, but probably more so at the very beginning. So, how can you make sure you're as prepared as possible?

CHAPTER 5

WHAT MORE CAN I DO TO

PREPARE FOR A POLICING CAREER?

At the start of every training course for prospective police recruits, I hold a discussion about what makes a good police officer. I ask what qualities they think you need to be a police officer and it always surprises me that there is usually one characteristic that is rarely mentioned. We usually hear about traits such as bravery, confidence and integrity as well as being a good communicator, approachable, unbiased and so on, but there is one that seems to escape most groups. They all seem to forget to mention honesty, but maybe that's because it's such an obvious one. I would hope that if you want to be a police officer, you already consider yourself an honest individual and generally apply honesty throughout your life. If you are already struggling with this basic principle required of each and every member of the force, then maybe look elsewhere for a career, as there is no place for outright dishonesty in a police officer.

Of course, it is not quite as straightforward as that and there is not a single police officer around who would say that they have never told a lie at some point in their life. In terms of carrying out your police duties, it is essential you are honest in upholding the law, preserving life and protecting the public. But what exactly does honesty mean and how does it apply specifically to a policing role?

In my view, it is absolutely essential that as a police officer you are open and truthful in carrying out your professional duty, especially in all dealings with the public. Whilst telling your supervisor you were late because the train was delayed when in reality you overslept has no great impact, telling this lie when you were late to be at a neighbourhood meeting could have a significant effect. If other people attending that meeting used the same train line or somehow found out you lied to them, they would understandably lose their trust in anything else you would say. Being honest is a key part of being a police officer, and preparing yourself for a policing role involves being honest with yourself and in all aspects of your professional life.

I have mentioned elsewhere the current fitness requirement for all serving police officers and there is a fitness test to be passed on an annual basis. I would suggest that good preparation before applying to become a police officer would include some form of physical exercise. The working hours can be long and the work can be stressful, so having a general good level of stamina will help you. As well as improving your physical fitness, I would also suggest taking an interest in current affairs and specifically police-related stories.

It always surprises me with a class of new recruits how little some of them know about the current issues affecting policing and some of the pivotal incidents or cases in police history. In the same way that you improve your physical condition by exercising, you should also improve your knowledge by exercising your mind. Read and learn about important cases over the years, like the Stephen Lawrence case, the Hillsborough inquiry, the 1981 Brixton riots and the serious disorder in 2011 after the shooting of Mark Duggan. Knowing about historic cases or incidents will also help you when studying legislation or changes in police working practices as they explain why certain new laws were passed. The Public Order Act 1986 was passed as a direct result of the serious disorders in 1981 and 1985 as until then different forces were using unbelievably ancient pieces of legislation that were only locally applicable. Indeed, in London, we were still operating according to the

Metropolitan Police Act 1839 to deal with disorder in 1981! The 1981 disorder in Brixton which spread to other parts of the UK also led to the Scarman report in 1981 and the Police and Criminal Evidence Act (PACE) in 1984. This one piece of legislation fundamentally changed important aspects of policing, including stopping and searching people and rules regarding arrest and detention. You cannot be a police officer without knowing PACE exceptionally well and applying it lawfully. It would be like wanting to be a professional footballer without understanding the offside rule or entering a well-known baking competition without ever trying to bake a cake. You absolutely need a basic understanding of policing history to effectively prepare yourself to become a police officer.

It would greatly help your preparation if you take some time to study policing over the last few decades. It isn't just about studying the laws and guidelines; you also need to learn about the police structure and how each rank functions. Knowing what a superintendent is and how senior they are could prevent a potentially embarrassing situation if you bumped into a senior officer on day one and greeted them with 'Hello, mate' or 'Morning, love' as opposed to 'sir' or 'ma'am'. Some promising police careers have been derailed or temporarily delayed due to failing to identify or correctly address their new boss on the first day.

Personal appearance is another one that some police recruits seem to struggle with and there are regulations about what is and isn't acceptable. In recent times, there has been debate about whether it is acceptable for police officers to have tattoos and, if so, to what extent. Personally, I don't have a problem with tattoos although I do not have any myself. I think each case must be judged individually, factoring in how many an officer has and whereabouts they are, but consider something I mentioned earlier about desirable qualities in police officers. Police officers need to be open, approachable and able to effectively communicate with the general public. Can an individual with numerous facial tattoos and possibly some that are offensive or frightening seem approachable, even when in a police uniform? If you are considering a police career and also getting a tattoo, then give some thought to where you have it placed and what it is. If you already have some that does not mean you cannot join, and most police forces these days are quite relaxed about them. You will be required to send in pictures of your existing tattoos for them to be assessed to see if they are suitable for a police officer.

The other contentious issue is length of hair for both sexes and facial hair for men. The phrase used in police regulations is 'neat and tidy', which means it should be off the collar for uniformed officers. Officers must tie any long hair into a bun so it is just off the collar and not in a ponytail, as it would then hang from underneath their hat. This may sound prohibitive, but in some cases it is essential and for your own safety. During any Public Order event and especially if you are deployed in full protective equipment along with the full-face protective helmet and visor, your hair is a safety issue. If it is hanging loose under the protective helmet, it could potentially be grabbed and used to pull you to the ground. It could also catch fire if any flammable objects are thrown at you and so, generally speaking, most operational or front-line female officers wear their hair up. Even on the so-called routine response policing role, having long hair is a safety issue. If you were called to deal with any sort of confrontation, your long hair is again a potential target for someone to grab hold of.

This is a copy of the current instructions from the Metropolitan Police for hair for potential recruits:

> Unless on identifiable religious grounds, hair must be worn above the collar. For safety reasons, ponytails are not permitted and long hair must be neatly and securely fastened up and worn close to the head (e.g. bun). Any hair bands or ties must be plain and the colour in-keeping with the main uniform. Students should seek the advice of staff if necessary. Hair must be neat and not be shaped or shaved into patterns or motifs. Moderate layering is acceptable but a sharp dividing line between long and

short sections of hair is not allowed. Hair must not be dyed in conspicuously 'unnatural' colours. With the exception of faint modest highlighting, hair may only be dyed one colour.

An 'unshaven' appearance is not permissible; therefore beards or moustaches must <u>not</u> be grown by students while in training. Students who have beards or moustaches when they join will be allowed to keep these provided they are neatly trimmed and comply with MPS policy on professional standards.

There is also a safety issue when it comes to jewellery and, again, you have to consider the problems that could arise if you are wearing long earrings. During your initial instruction, the training staff will insist that you only wear small studs at most. There may be some relaxation on this, especially if you move into a different policing role, but front-line or response policing attracts its own risks. The current directions for body jewellery are as follows: 'rings, studs or sleepers must not be worn through the ears, nose, eyebrows, tongue or any other visible part of the body. Staff who have body piercings that are not visible when clothed should be aware of the associated risk of injury and remove jewellery as necessary.'

It is a similar rule with excessive make up and again, during training, your instructors will remind you that excessive make up is not acceptable for uniformed officers. The police guidelines for cosmetics are: 'Cosmetics may be worn in moderation and should be appropriate to the work environment. Nails must be kept to a length that will not interfere with duties. Any nail varnish worn must be colourless.'

That must all sound fairly draconian, but the important aspect is trying to maintain a uniformed or corporate image for the police service whilst also looking approachable to the public. Individuality can still be maintained, but the nature of the profession means it is important that appearance is kept low-key. As with most occupations and jobs, the guidance in any training course seems to become relaxed once you qualify or pass. I can remember seeing some female officers with bright red lipstick and I always knew when they were on duty as the tea mugs had pink marks on the rims. The only time I worried was when I found the mugs with the lipstick marks on them and none of the ladies were on duty! Our resident scenes of crime officer did offer to 'forensically examine' said marks, but for some reason our sergeant declined the request.

The most difficult aspect to try and prepare for is arguably the shift work and stresses of the job. Hopefully, you will have already realised that policing is a 24/7 job, and so it does mean that you will at some point have to work all night. I have known some recruits who joined and were under the misapprehension that special units did the whole night and most police officers finished by midnight. Working nights is hard and it is not natural to force your body to stay awake all night and then go to bed in the morning. Your whole body-clock and routine is disrupted and one of the most difficult things to balance is your eating habits. Consider for a moment getting up at 4 p.m. if you are lucky to sleep that long, then maybe having breakfast – but you are not at work for another six hours, so at what time do you have a main meal? Maybe skip breakfast then have your main meal at 7 p.m. before going to work for a 10 p.m. start? The other option is to have breakfast when you get up and then main meal at 2 a.m. whilst at work, but that just feels really odd. In short, you will need to find out what works best for you – and that's just whilst you are performing duty.

Then there is the whole day before you start your first night; do you sleep part of the day or all through the day? Trying to sleep during the daytime in the summer when everyone is out in their gardens, cutting grass, and the rest of the world seems to be awake is really challenging. You will be the odd one out trying to sleep when it is 27 degrees outside, with brilliant sunshine streaming through your curtains. There will also be added interruptions to your slumber with postmen rattling your letterbox and delivery people calling. To put it simply: it is very hard. Shift patterns differ across police forces in the UK. When I started we used to work seven nights in a row from Monday to Sunday but the more common shift patterns these days are three or four nights in a row, but after the last night shift you return to work later the same day. You may finish and be in bed at 6 a.m. and then up again around 1 p.m. to be back at work that afternoon for a late shift. Other places may have a rest day after your last night, so you finish at 6 a.m. and you are off all that day. This brings a separate problem, as having a rest day after your last night means you spend most of it in bed sleeping, unless you force yourself to get up mid-morning. The alternative is you sleep until the afternoon having finished at 6 a.m. but you are then still wide awake at 3 a.m. whilst the rest of the house is asleep. Your body-clock has become so used to being awake all night that even though you are on a day off, you stay awake and end up watching endless movie re-runs through the night (I recommend *Blues Brothers* and *Animal House*!).

So, how can you prepare for this? I am not about to suggest you try to make yourself nocturnal and start eating at odd hours of the day. Staying in bed until the afternoon seems to suit most teenagers, but I found adapting to shift work surprisingly tough when I first started in policing aged nineteen. It is not easy, but there are some positives to it and I will outline just a few. At night, most of the bosses are in bed so the station effectively belongs to you and your team and you have a whole shift to deal with incidents. You will not get calls overnight from the administration departments or paperwork processing units about outstanding forms or case files as, like most normal people, they are all in bed. You will not receive enquiries from the Crown Prosecution Service about court cases or witness statements as again, they are sound asleep. Outside of policing, there are other positives to working nights. You can get to the shops during the day without fighting to park or queuing for the check-out. The gym is quiet as most people are at work, as are the pubs and restaurants. It is quite amazing how much opens up to you when you are working nights, providing you can get out of bed before the mid-afternoon. Whilst there are some positives to working nights, there is only so much you can do to prepare yourself and going clubbing or staying out all night isn't really the best form of preparation for a policing career. It comes back to being healthy and fit and considering when and what you are going to eat and then finding what works best for you.

I have said this would be an honest guide about how to be a police officer, and so I have to say that there is no easy way to deal with the stresses of the job. We each have our own personal experiences and some unpleasant memories may be repeated during your policing career in similar situations and it is understandable that memories may return and possibly cause you additional stress. You have to remain professional and try and place your own feelings to one side in order to effectively deal with whatever you are facing. In some instances, your own experiences may help you to understand and empathise with whoever or whatever you are dealing with. The key here is to accept you will face stressful situations and acknowledge you have to deal with them. Do not be afraid of identifying when the stress is becoming too difficult to cope with and recognising when you may need help. The police service knows that officers may need help in relation to dealing with stress and there have been improvements in the support available. It is by no means a perfect support structure, but it is important that you are aware of the impact of stress and ask for help or support.

So, our preparation includes increasing physical exercise and paying particular attention to any police-related stories. Consider waiting until you have completed your training before getting any new tattoos on exposed parts of your body. Decide if your long hair is worth putting up and leaving under a hat every day. Explain to your family and loved ones that policing is not a 9–5 weekday-only occupation and that there may be an empty chair at the Christmas table some years. This is not a definitive or exhaustive list by any means; it just means that you should be aware that being a police officer requires you to consider making some lifestyle changes.

Having started to make these changes in your lifestyle, how exactly do you apply to be a police officer and what is involved in the training and assessment days?

CHAPTER 6

ASSESSMENT DAYS AND

INITIAL TRAINING

Long before you reach your assessment day, you will need to apply to join the police. This can be a long and drawn-out process, but I'm sure you will realise that selecting people to become police officers should not be easy or quick. The initial application form contains a lot of questions about your personal details and educational qualifications. You should make sure you have the relevant identification documents in your possession to make completing the form a lot easier. Once that has been submitted you will hopefully be invited to attend an assessment day. Some forces are now using an online questionnaire that presents you with questions about how you would approach different scenarios as part of their selection process.

The content and duration of recruit assessment may differ slightly from force to force but they are all likely to last one or two days and will involve some aptitude tests, a competency-based interview and some form of role play assessment. The test is taken by all applicants and involves verbal reasoning and numerical ability tests. Be prepared to be asked difficult questions about your views and beliefs and how they compare with the qualities of being a police officer. Some companies provide assessment day training workshops where you can practise the questions, role plays and interviews. Most applicants find the role plays and interviews the most challenging parts as the content is always a surprise. In the role plays, the workshop will likely ask you to play the role of a customer service manager rather than a police officer. Some people find this strange, but the reasoning behind this is simple. You are not a police officer, so they cannot accurately assess you in that role or expect you to know how to deal with a scenario as a police officer. In contrast, all of us have been a customer at some point and have had an issue that needed to be resolved by someone in authority. The assessment centre is there to test your ability when it comes to working with other people, how well you explain yourself and communicate with other people and whether you can focus on the key points. Successful applicants will be courteous, considerate, polite and able to empathise with others. They will also be looking to see if you treat people respectfully whilst also taking ownership of the issue, even though you may not be able to resolve it there and then, and explain what you will do and why. Practise your communication skills, including the ability to actively listen, by watching TV interviews or news programmes. Maintain eye contact and nod occasionally to show you are paying attention, and then summarise what you have been told to show them you have understood what they have said. At the assessment centre you will have time to read a briefing that explains your role, who you are seeing and the issue they want to talk about. Keep an open mind when you are dealing with the role plays as the initial issue mentioned may not be the real problem, so you may need to ask some probing and open-ended questions such as 'Why has this happened? Is there anything else going on? Describe to me exactly and in detail what happened.'

The role plays can feel slightly false, but they are incredibly important when it comes to assessing your ability to communicate and deal with people, which is a fundamental skill required of all police officers.

As well as the role plays and tests, you will also have a competency-based interview. This usually lasts around twenty minutes and will cover skills like decision making, working with others, serving the public, openness to change, professionalism and service delivery. You will be asked to provide examples of how you have dealt with specific incidents in the past. This is where you can take control of the interview to a certain extent, as it is all about your own knowledge and experience. Pick a good example of a situation where you have had to deal with something that was challenging and try to make it relevant to a policing role. Use an example that shows your strengths, not one where someone else did all the talking and resolved the issue. This is about you and you are trying to demonstrate that you have the basic qualities to become a police officer. I have to add a little mnemonic here to help you remember what you need in the competency-based interview. STAR stands for situation, task, action and result. This means you should explain the situation as fully as you can before setting out what your task was, what actions you took and the overall result. Personalise it as much as possible, so use 'I' as opposed to 'we' in your explanation so the assessors understand that this was you dealing with the situation. Tell them exactly what you did, and how you communicated that to the other persons involved. Explain your reasoning in the situation in such a way that if the assessors close their eyes, they can visualise you dealing with the incident as you explain it.

That effectively sums up an assessment day and although the timetables may differ from force to force, they mostly all use the same framework and content. Some forces, including the Metropolitan, have a second assessment day where your fitness is assessed and you undergo some basic medical tests. You will also have to take a drugs test, which is often done by cutting approximately 100 strands of hair from your head. You will be expected to provide your fingerprints which are now taken by an electronic machine, so no more ink pads and rolling the fingers in the ink, although it's worth knowing how to do it as that method is still used if the machine doesn't work. The old-fashioned way to take fingerprints was to put some blobs of ink from a tube onto a brass plate which was fixed onto a chest-high wooden table. You'd then roll out the ink blobs until the entire brass plate was covered. Once you had the surface entirely covered in this thin layer of ink, you then had to prepare the paper fingerprint form – and that was the fun part. You had to fold it in a certain way in three places so only those parts of the form that you needed were showing: a sort-of police origami test. The form was secured to the table by placing it under a metal bracket alongside the now thinly inked plate. Each finger had a corresponding box on the form, starting with the right index finger until all four boxes for the right hand were complete. It was essential that for this first impression the finger was rolled across the brass plate and then rolled again on the paper form. You had to roll it, as just pressing down left you with an inky smudge. You then moved the form up in its retaining bracket so the boxes for the left hand were visible and repeated the process with the left fingers. Lastly, the form was moved up again to the third and last fold for the plain impressions of all four fingers and this was taken at a slight angle. Once again you took all four fingers on the right hand but pressed them down together and then pressed down on the ink plate to get the plain impressions. Carefully moving over to your form, you turned the four fingers at a slight angle so they all fitted into the appropriate box and pressed down. This was repeated for the left-hand fingers on the opposite side of the form and between these were two boxes for the plain impressions of both thumbs. You were also left with a person with very inky hands who needed to wash them quickly before they used your pen to sign the form!

Back in those days, fingerprint ink played a key role in many practical jokes in police stations, with the telephone earpiece or the inside of a colleague's hat being regularly inked up for an unsuspecting user. The tell-tale ink ring around an ear or across the forehead gave the game away and the sniggers of your colleagues as you walked past them were an even bigger clue. Luckily technology has overtaken the practical jokers. Whilst ink is rarely used these days when taking fingerprints, most police stations still retain some paper forms together with ink and the fingerprint platform. They are a standby for any technology failing and can be used to take elimination prints at locations away from a police station. No doubt as technology improves, hand-held scanners will be developed and paper and ink will be consigned to history and the bottom of old police lockers.

You will also have to provide a DNA sample at some point and together with the fingerprints these are checked to ensure you have no outstanding offences or criminal record. The fingerprints and DNA are retained as they will need to be kept for elimination purposes when you eventually work as a police officer. Imagine a confrontational situation where a struggle ensues and you need to use force or maybe you inadvertently touch objects linked to the crime. Your own prints and DNA will be all over the scene and on the objects, so when they are forensically examined your marks can quickly be eliminated and the investigation team will be left with just the suspect's prints and DNA.

After your assessment day(s), you then wait for a date to start. These dates are governed by a number of factors, which include the number of recruits required at that time by that particular police force, and availability of training centres, classrooms and sufficient staff to train the recruits. I have spoken to numerous recruits in different forces and found that the waiting time to join after completing the assessment day varies, but it is roughly three to six months, although a few have waited longer on some occasions.

The duration of the initial training can vary, but it is

usually around thirteen weeks and is non-residential for almost all police forces now, so you travel to and from the training centre each day. Depending on the numbers being trained, most days are 9–5, but some of the larger forces like the Metropolitan Police will run classes over two shifts between 7 a.m. and 10 p.m. This means your training class could be 7 a.m. to 3 p.m. for one week and then 2 p.m. until 10 p.m. the following week and alternate throughout your course. The initial training can differ in structure and detail from force to force, but the constant factor will be learning the legislation and how to apply it. This involves some classroom time together with lots of practice in the much-loved role plays. At this stage of training, instructors will play the part of members of the public who may have called police and you will be assessed as you investigate and deal with the incident.

There are some multiple-choice exams that you must pass during your training and there has been a slight change in their format. Most of the police service has moved away from the kind of questions where you had to choose a combination of three or four separate answers. This is because it took too long to read all the answers to a multiple-choice question. The majority of forces now only have four options to the multiple-choice questions in an exam that will test your detailed knowledge of the legislation you have learnt. As with most multiple-choice tests, there are usually one or two answers you can dismiss straight away and then you are left with two that look probable. The devil is in the detail here, as they are testing your literal understanding of the legislation and for some you need to know every word of an offence or at least the points to prove being made. Take a charge of criminal damage as an example; you would need to know the full definition of the offence, the specific wording used to describe the offence, which must include the words damaged or destroyed, intentional or reckless, and state that it is concerning property belonging to another damaged without lawful excuse. A typical question about criminal damage in the exam might give you the following answer options: damaged or demolished, or damaged or devastated, or the correct option of damaged or destroyed. Your knowledge, therefore, needs to be detailed when it comes to correctly identifying the essential points to prove of each offence you have learnt. When I did my initial training, I learnt all the charges word for word by writing them down on postcard-sized memos and carrying them around with me so I could read and learn them in any spare moments. I still advise this method to any recruits I teach as the more often you see and read something, the better it seems that you are able to remember it.

It seems one of the most sought-after pieces of information about what the initial training will be like concerns the officer safety training (OST). Many recruits I have taught seem keen to find out when they will start their OST and when they will receive their handcuffs, baton, incapacitant spray etc. I have no idea what drives this apparent desire to be handcuffed twelve times in an hour or have a training baton whacked across a pad that you are holding. OST is a national programme so, regardless of which police force you join, you should receive the standardised training. You will be taken through empty-hand skills to teach you to strike using your hands. You will also be trained in leg strikes and some basic self-defence moves and tactics to give you an understanding of how to defend yourself. The key part of this aspect of your training is that you know the law in relation to using force, when you can justify it and what is considered reasonable force. At every OST session I attended – and we were required to be trained twice a year – we were reminded of the law in relation to using force, which states that each individual strike or application of force must be reasonable and justified. That does not mean to say this is the only form of self-defence you can use. If you have a particular skill in martial arts or self-defence you can use those but, again, it's all about being reasonable and justified in the circumstances.

Can you actually punch someone as a police officer? If you can justify that level of force and it is reasonable in the circumstances, then yes. The law is quite clear about self-defence in respect of assault and it focuses on whether each individual instance was reasonable and justified. The actual OST also involves you pairing up with your colleagues and practising handcuffing each other. Expect to go home from any OST with sore and painful wrists after your colleagues learn to apply some 'pain compliance'. A helpful hint here is to always go second on any handcuff practice as then you will know how vigorously your partner has applied them before it is your turn! The same goes for the baton strikes you will practise, which involves one of you holding the pad whilst the other practises their strikes. Remember to try and pay attention to what your colleague with the baton is doing. In almost every OST session there is the occasional 'ouch!' or more extreme expletive used, as the pad-holder isn't always paying attention and receives a high or low strike after failing to move the pad in time.

Lastly, you will be trained in using whatever incapacitant spray your force uses. The Metropolitan Police use CS spray or, to use its technical name, 2-Chlorobenzalmalononitrile. You will be exposed to a diluted form of the spray during training and that's when you will discover any intolerance to the spray. I found it turns me into a sneezing, sniffling and eyes-streaming wreck that is almost incapable of coherent speech – although some of my students may claim that's what I'm usually like. I decided after training that I would never carry my issued CS spray because it can have a worse effect on the user than on the suspect. The spray contains minute crystals that react with the air and can spread to anyone nearby. It is not effective on some people, especially those experiencing heightened excitement due to drink or drugs. I decided I would leave mine in my locker as, knowing my luck, the one time I used it the effect would be on me rather than my intended target. I am not advocating you do the same and I know many officers who have used it very effectively in confrontational situations. You do have to check it every day as the canister needs agitating to keep the chemicals reactive and the crystals mixed. You achieve this by holding the canister between your fore-finger and thumb, gently shaking it backwards and forwards. Think of the gesture many football fans make with their finger and thumb, moving them from side to side towards the referee or the opposing fans, and you have it.

Your initial training, then, is a balance between testing your already-acquired knowledge of the theory of policing, including the laws, policies and guidelines, and your practical application of this understanding. There are also practical assessments that you need to pass, including stopping and searching someone and dealing with a drink-drive incident in which you administer a breath test. You will receive instruction and can practise these in class with your fellow recruits, but all the assessments must be passed before you can move on from your basic initial training.

You have now been through your initial training and are about to be sent out onto the streets; but what uniform are you given and is there anything else you may need to buy yourself?

CHAPTER 7

WHAT UNIFORM DO I GET?

This might sound like a strange question; surely the police provide you with all the uniform you need for the job and nothing else is required? Well, it turns out that one of the most commonly asked questions at all of the training courses I have taught on is about the uniform they receive.

Try to picture a police officer in uniform and then consider what you imagine is part of all the issued kit. A hat may come to mind first and, yes, you will be issued with two of these: one for when you are out on foot patrol and one for patrolling in a car. Why do you need two different styles of hat? The traditional hat is called the custodian helmet, which is uniquely shaped and referred to within the service as 'the tit' for obvious reasons due to its shape. It is completely unsuitable for patrol in a car due its size, as it is about a foot high. The original custodian helmets were made from cork and were extremely lightweight and much easier to wear on your head for prolonged periods of time than the current ones. When I joined, the older cork style was very much sought after by us newer constables but they afforded no protection whatsoever. The modern ones are made from a very strong plastic covered with a water-repellent wool material with the inside harness and chin strap attached and the Force insignia badge on the front of the helmet. There's a YouTube clip showing how these helmets are made if you are interested.

There is also quite a well-known urban myth that pregnant women are legally allowed to urinate into a police officer's helmet if there are no other toilet facilities available nearby. I heard this rumour for many years and so when researching this book, I searched for the relevant legislation that would allow this bizarre incident to take place – and I still remain unsure of its truth. I cannot find it referenced anywhere despite several mentions on various public forums that it exists and that it is very, very old. Considering the factors for this to happen: that the lady in question must be in urgent need to urinate and be pregnant, there are no public toilets in the area and the police officer is wearing a helmet, then after all that why would any pregnant woman want to wee into your hat! I would suggest if you receive any such request that it is politely declined and you direct any pregnant lady enquiring about this 'facility' to the nearest toilet.

Along with your traditional helmet, you will also receive a flat cap that is predominantly used for the times you are deployed on mobile patrol in a police vehicle. There have been recent discussions by some about discontinuing the use and provision of the custodian helmet and only issuing the flat caps, in order to save costs. The current situation is that Thames Valley and West Yorkshire forces have discontinued issuing the helmet, and in Scotland it is no longer issued at all. In the last few weeks whilst writing this, there has been talk of re-issuing helmets in Thames Valley and retaining them across the UK, and the reason given for changing the decision to withdraw them is quite strange. There is no height restriction when joining the police service these days, and it seems that some senior officers have now decided that having a foot-high helmet on your head is beneficial as it makes you more visible on patrol. Nothing to do with affording you more protection: it's just so that people will see officers more easily, which is definitely advantageous if you are under 5ft 10in. tall. A visible police service makes the public more confident, so it would seem the traditional custodian police helmet may be staying after all.

A fairly recent addition to the uniform has been the issue of baseball caps to certain specialised police units, as they are light and easy to store. Some plain-clothes police units will have police-issue baseball caps for the incidents where they have to identify themselves as police officers, as they can be easily stored in a pocket until required. Firearms units and tactical support groups also issue police baseball caps, which can be easily removed and replaced with the protective helmet when dealing with public disorder incidents.

Police officers will always have at least one of the issued hats when on patrol, whether in a vehicle or on foot. Whenever you leave your vehicle, you will be expected to put your hat on. Sometimes officers are rebuked for not wearing their hat by senior officers who happen to be passing by as the officer is dealing with an incident. This always bemuses me as, on most occasions, there is a very valid reason for not taking the time to put your hat back on … like chasing a suspect! Never mind if you have just detained a suspect after a lengthy foot-chase across gardens and roads, the first question asked by the passing senior officer would be, 'Why aren't you wearing your hat, officer?' A helpful tip would be to always have a good excuse ready and, from experience, merely waving a handcuffed suspect under their nose isn't always the answer.

What about your police-issue trousers? Most forces now issue cargo-type trousers which have pockets on the thighs and are usually fairly baggy in style and fit. I accept I may have an old-fashioned view and that their practicality is more important than how they look, but most officers look considerably less smart in these new trousers than they ever did in the old style. I can only assume it is down to cost and the cargo trousers must be cheaper. Police officers do have to carry around numerous books and forms on their patrol so, in all fairness, there is a need for a uniform with sufficient pockets that can also withstand inclement weather and general wear and tear. I just wish they were smarter looking or more tailored. I have seen some forces with the cargo-style uniform trouser, but the style they use are a much better fit and look smart. These tailored types of cargo trousers mean that it is still possible not to look scruffy whilst still being practical. Regardless of the style, you will be given at least two pairs of trousers and, as it is a uniformed service, you cannot wear your own version, even if they are more comfortable or better fitting.

What about shirts? You will be issued with a shirt or top to wear depending on which force you join. Scotland is now covered by one police force, Police Scotland, and they receive the plain black T-shirt that was pioneered by Strathclyde Police in 2003. This was a slightly controversial move at the time as it looked too sinister or para-military to some. Some critics even likened it to the uniform of Oswald Moseley, but it is now being adopted by many other forces as it is a more practical style and colour of shirt. The Metropolitan Police still issue white shirts and they were the only ones to wear white shirts when I first joined. The Met have moved on to a more practical white shirt and now also have a short-sleeved white polo shirt that fits much better under the stab-proof vest. We are now seeing many forces move towards this polo style short-sleeved shirt and some are favouring the black variety as opposed to the traditional white colour. They can all be worn with the stab-proof vest over the top, which is much more comfortable than wearing a traditional button up collared shirt. The black-coloured shirts are not only far more comfortable to wear, but they are less visible at night, which hopefully makes catching suspects in the dark much easier. You will receive usually three or more shirts and they are now of the non-iron type to make cleaning and wearing them much easier, although I have yet to find a police-issue non-iron shirt that looks like it doesn't need ironing after it has been washed!

The most commonly asked question about the uniform issued when you join the police is about footwear. You are not issued with shoes or boots when you first join, so you must select and purchase your own footwear. You will, however, be issued with Public Order boots should you ever progress into being a Public Order trained officer, but on first joining you need to organise your own footwear. The Public Order boots have re-enforced toecaps and soles so they can withstand petrol bombing or objects thrown at police, but that is not a requirement for your general patrol boots.

So, what boots should you buy and when should you get them? Let's look at a couple of provisions first: they must be plain and black with no fancy stitching or patterns on the boot or shoe. I would suggest a very comfortable pair of boots that you can walk in for some distance and stand still in for long periods of time. There are numerous companies offering 'police-issue boots' and they all advertise in various police magazines and on police websites. You can spend a lot of money on top-quality boots and, obviously, it all depends on your own personal financial situation, but for your first pair I would suggest a moderately priced pair. I always found it difficult to drive in my issue Public Order boots due to the rigidity of the actual boot and the width and strength of the sole. I used to drive in a pair of plain black shoes when I was a front-line response officer and have my boots in a kit bag. If we were called to an incident involving serious disorder, I would change into my boots whilst putting on my overalls and Public Order helmet. Ideally, try to wear the boots in for a bit before attempting to walk around in them on an eight-hour foot patrol. Wearing them during training is a good tip so you become used to them and they will then be comfortable when you first go out on patrol. You will have more than enough to think about on your first few days without worrying about blisters on your feet.

The modern types of boots available now are more flexible

and durable, so you have a greater choice than the almost solitary Doc Martens I was faced with in the early days. It used to be difficult to actually find plain black ones as the favoured option in the late '70s and early '80s was a cherry-red DM boot. It always seemed ironic that many of the football hooligans we dealt with were wearing the same type of footwear as most of the cops. Whenever we were on football duty, the officers searching the fans entering the ground were required to test the fans' boots as they entered the turnstiles. Doc Martens offered a steel toecap version of their boot and this seemed to be the preferred 'weapon' of choice for many involved in football violence. To combat this tactic, police officers were deployed to search fans' pockets thoroughly whilst they stood in the queue for the turnstile and then ask, 'Are they steels, mate?' Regardless of the answer, you would test their boot by standing on the toecap and if that was met with a slight grimace or yelp, they were allowed to pass. If, however, they stayed firm and the toecap withstood your own size-nine pressing firmly down, you demanded they remove their boot laces and surrendered them before entering the ground. I remember performing this role at my own favourite team's ground, Stamford Bridge, the home of Chelsea FC. Alongside the old turnstiles at the entrance to the infamous 'Shed End' was a long drainpipe and, by the time kick off came, it was usually covered in a variety of boot laces surrendered by supporters who had tried to enter wearing their favourite steel toecaps. I am not sure how many of the laces were ever successfully reunited with their owners, or whether it became a sort of unofficial boot lace swap-shop. I am convinced it was here that the fashion for having different coloured or non-matching laces was born. Funnily enough, the yellow coloured laces were always the ones still on the drainpipe when the police officers walked away.

Now you're in possession of your issue hats, shirts and trousers, and you have trawled the internet and shoe shops for your chosen footwear – so what else do you need to know?

Most forces these days realise that police officers need a functional, comfortable and practical uniform to wear on the streets. The iconic tunic, whistle chain, helmet and suit-type trousers may look smart and presentable, but are far from practical. That type of uniform is great for any events when police officers are lining a ceremonial route, such as Trooping the Colour or Remembrance Sunday.

For a late shift where you may have to work in the wind and rain or chase suspects across parks or fields, you will be issued with a fleece top. The type and style of jacket you will receive to wear over your fleece and body armour, be it an anorak or a coat, is dependent on which force you join. These are usually Gore-Tex, so they are allegedly waterproof and wind resistant, but remember this is police-issue kit, so don't expect miracles.

You will also receive a high visibility (fluorescent yellow) jacket to wear over your issued black anorak. Some forces and departments issue an all-in-one high-vis coat so the jacket is already fluorescent yellow. Think of traffic or motorway officers, who predominantly wear this due to the type of policing work they do and the need to be highly visible. Most patrol officers have a thinner high-vis jacket that goes over the top of their issued anorak or fleece when they are performing a specific role or at an incident that requires greater visibility. The issued stab-proof vest is made up of layers of Kevlar material. This has an outer cover with the black police logo on it, and the inner Kevlar layered insert can be removed from the outer cover and washed, although not many officers seem to bother with that. You will also be issued with some black leather gloves which are an absolute gift from heaven in the winter months.

As a guide, the current issue uniform in the Metropolitan Police Service includes the following:

One pair of white cotton gloves
One pair of black leather gloves
Six white shirts
Two pairs of cargo-style trousers
Tunic jacket and trousers (no.1 uniform for ceremonial duty)
Two sets of epaulettes (these are the shoulder identification tabs)
Two cravats (women) or two ties (men)

Two name tags (you can decide how you are identified either PC then your surname or both first name and surname)

Gore-Tex style black anorak

Black woollen fleece

High-visibility jacket (fluorescent yellow)

Waterproof over-trousers (similar to the type golfers wear)

Stab-proof Met vest,

Kit belt (this is a clip fastening equipment belt to carry your PPE equipment on including handcuffs, baton, first aid pouch, CS spray holder)

A normal belt for your trousers

Four belt attachments

The total cost is approximately £140.

Is there anything missing?

Pens! Only black ink is allowed to be used on police forms and I would always advocate having a couple of spare pens every time you go out on patrol. It would look unprofessional if whilst reporting an incident your pen runs out. I know technology is advancing and possibly in a few years' time reports will be written on electronic tablets, but there will always be a need for old fashioned pen and paper.

What else would be useful then? We used to get issued with a torch with the illumination power of a candle that was about to go out. They really were poor and the slightest hint of rain meant they stopped working; drop them once and they stopped working; shake them to try to get light and they stopped working. Mine lasted about a week, which was not bad going by all accounts. I have seen police officers who are clearly so obsessed with kit and equipment and have so many pouches and holders on their belt, it's amazing they can walk. Some also seem obsessed with having the biggest torch they can possess ... no jokes here about size matters, but remember you have to carry it around and actually use it. I would suggest buying a decent torch that is designed to be used outdoors, not too big in size and can fit in your pocket. You do not want one of these four-cell or six-cell types that thuds against your knee every time you move. You will need a decent torch even though it might be tempting just to use the app on your phone, as that requires having your phone out and in your hand and that is far from safe or recommended practice for an officer. A torch that provides good illumination, is comfortable and convenient to carry but can be secured on your belt to leave your hands free would be ideal.

Next, you need a decent-sized rucksack or kit bag to carry the numerous forms, spare pens and other equipment you may need when out on a vehicle patrol. This is entirely down to personal choice, but like everything else it should be predominantly black in colour. You are not going on holiday or camping overnight in the woods, so make sure it isn't too big and limit how much you put in the bag.

There are guidelines outlining what personal items you should carry whilst at work, and we have seen some of these in an earlier chapter. The rules recognise that policing is a risky occupation and that wearing expensive personal items is not the best idea. The official guidelines contain the following warning:

> Expensive personal items, including jewellery, must not be worn at work. A plain watch, items of religious significance and no more than two rings may be worn. Rings with prominent stones or settings must not be worn on duty, because of the risk of injury. Necklaces must not be visible.

I own two very nice watches that were both presents and I would never consider wearing either of them whilst policing, due to the high possibility of damaging them. I purchased a fairly cheap (£30) but functional watch with a Velcro fastening to wear whilst on patrol and at Public Order events. You will need to have a watch as timings are crucial for operational policing duties, from noting the time of arrival at a call to time of arrest or caution of a suspect. Sometimes, an entire case may hinge on the time at which a suspect was seen or detained by police, or when the actual offence took place. A watch is probably one of the most important pieces of equipment you will need, but they are not supplied so choose carefully and frugally. A watch with a luminous dial is also a very helpful bonus, as it is often dark whilst you are policing. Try to avoid the bracelet type of fastening, as these can easily become unfastened during any struggle if someone grabs your wrist. I used to wear this type of watch until this exact thing happened to me and my watch was rattling round my wrist whilst I was struggling to detain someone. I eventually had to flick the watch off my wrist as it was preventing me from securing the suspect, and it crashed to the floor. Its enthusiastically claimed 'shock proof' guarantee sadly did not seem to cover it being flung forcefully off my wrist during a struggle with a violent suspect. Hence my move to the traditional strap type with a Velcro fastening to secure the watch to my wrist.

One last story about uniform. It's a cautionary tale, although it does prove the versatility of police uniform. Whilst I was working at Scotland Yard in 2006, my unit was deployed to York to assist North Yorkshire police as part of the climate camp policing contingent at the Drax power station. We were there for a week's deployment, so we had to take sufficient uniform for the duration of our stay. We arrived in York late in the evening and our first briefing and deployment was at 7 a.m. the next morning. My room-mate Steve and I were tasked with the job of managing and briefing our teams. Our alarms were set for 5.15 a.m. so that we would have sufficient time to get ready. I was up first and, as I put on my uniform,

I noticed Steve was swearing as he rummaged through the wardrobe. He appeared from behind the door with a pair of dark coloured trousers, but even at 5.15 a.m. I could tell that they were not police issue uniform trousers. A moderately smart pair of navy blue suit-trousers was hanging from his arms, and I could just make out the 'Topman' label on the waistband.

'Bollocks, I picked up the wrong trousers from my locker', he astutely realised. As one of our foremost police forward intelligence officers with an encyclopaedic ability to recognise faces and people, he seemed to have cocked up when 'identifying' his uniform trousers from his dancing ones! I suggested that maybe he had brought a spare pair with him since Drax power station was in the middle of rural countryside and it was highly likely we would spend most of our days walking through fields and footpaths; but for some reason, he had decided to pack one pair of trousers as he never considered we might be getting muddy every day!

I had the foresight to pack a spare pair of trousers (that's why I was the sergeant!), but sadly they did not fit him as he couldn't do them up. My suggestion that he should have salad for breakfast did not help the situation. The only solution was to ask if anyone had a spare pair of uniform trousers and if they would fit Steve. Police officers do come in all shapes and sizes but it seemed that out of our twenty-strong contingent none were the same shape and size as Steve. There was just one glimmer of hope as John had a spare pair of trousers but astonishingly he also encountered a similar mishap. He had taken a spare pair of uniform trousers from his ironing pile at home, but his wife was also a serving police officer and he inadvertently picked up her trousers.

Accompanied by John and a few other helpful observers, we collected the spare pair of ladies' police-issue trousers and handed them over. Steve was not overly impressed but he had to try them on. It turned out that they fitted him! Steve eventually came into the breakfast room and was greeted by various shouts of 'Morning, Stephanie' and 'Hello, gorgeous!' as he collected his food, which astonishingly wasn't salad or fruit. He told us that he actually preferred the ladies trousers as they had a padded crotch area and then began stretching and tapping said area to demonstrate the added padding. John looked less than impressed with this description and associated touching of his wife's clothing and vowed he would 'lose' them before he returned home. The vital lesson is to make sure you check that everything you need is in your kit bag if you are working at another station or different location. If the worst does happen and you do forget an item then have no fear; it seems that many parts of police uniform are unisex and interchangeable, although maybe keep the fact you are wearing them to yourself.

So, equipped with your full police uniform as issued by your force and ensuring you have suitable footwear, some pens, a rucksack or bag, a torch and a cheap, functional watch, you are ready for the big wide world of policing.

After this, what happens when you finally reach an operational police station and work with experienced police officers and start the job for real?

CHAPTER 8

DAY ONE AT A POLICE STATION

Whilst your trainers will have used all the modern technology available, such as computers and videos to simulate police-type scenarios, you cannot really replicate the real working life as a police officer. Your training to date will have been theory-based for the CKP and then you will have applied that knowledge into practical scenarios during your initial training. All of this will have been mainly carried out in classroom environments under the watchful gaze of trainers, assessors and your fellow police recruits. Your officer safety training will be carried out in a safe and controlled environment, where you will use training batons and protective pads to prevent any serious injuries. Once you have successfully passed the theory assessments, practical role plays and officer safety training, you will be sent to your first police station and 'introduced' to the public. On your first day, you will meet the senior officer in charge of your area who will formally welcome you and explain what they expect from you as a police officer.

Turning up and having a chat with the boss sounds fairly easy, but you also need to remember a few other factors that will complicate the day for you. You will need to bring your full patrol uniform with you in a kit bag, including two hats, trousers, shirts, belt, handcuffs and ASP/baton to name but a few, as officers do not travel to work in uniform. You will arrive prepared to patrol and work for the whole day as a professional police officer with all the equipment and uniform that role entails. You will be allocated a locker in the police station which will become the home for all your uniform for as long as you are working there. There are some items you will take home, including your shirts and anything else that may need laundering or dry cleaning, but most operational officers leave everything else at work. There are usually irons and an ironing board around most locker rooms, although the iron's effectiveness is sometimes questionable. You should never use the steam function as you will undoubtedly witness a jet of mucky brown liquid propel onto your clean clothing. Irons in police stations are usually neglected so at best they can just about press an item of clothing, but do not expect anything else. You may even have to iron your clothes with the board laid flat on the floor as the legs will have broken. The iron itself is also likely to have substances melted onto its surface not yet identified by NASA scientists. You will first discover this at 5.30 a.m. when you are ironing your shirt for duty and, as you peel the iron away, it leaves a black molten mess somewhere near the neck. It is never low down where it can be hidden under your protective vest, as that would make things far too easy. I have no idea what some police officers choose to iron at work to leave this congealed mass stuck to the face of most irons. It is particularly frustrating because this molten muck only appears when the iron is hot, so it looks fine at first glance. You may have guessed that it is usually best to wash and iron your uniform clothing in the comfort of your own home and then bring it into work.

Why is this important? You will have spent some of your initial training being inspected to make sure that both you and your uniform look professional. Are the public likely to approach you or have confidence in you if you look like you have slept in your uniform? I doubt they would, and it is down to you to ensure your uniform always looks clean and tidy. You will be issued with spare shirts and trousers as, inevitably, you will get dirty whilst patrolling and dealing with incidents. Dog handlers or mounted branch officers arguably have an even tougher job to keep clean and tidy, as they are working alongside a partner that sheds large quantities of hair and requires regular walks through fields and woods. The dog handler or mounted officer might start the day looking clean and smart, but give it just one call or maybe an exercise walk for the dog and they look like they have completed a Tough Mudder. That is usually the exact moment they come face-to-face with one of the senior officers and receive the inevitable rebuke about failing to look professional as they stand there covered in mud and fur. Operational policing is carried out in all weathers and in all sorts of areas, and you will get muddy and dirty during your working hours. The key here is to take the time before or after work to make sure you have clean uniform and boots/shoes for your next shift. There are numerous stories about police officers – usually the men – wearing the same shirt on consecutive days and resorting to putting Tipp-Ex on the collars of their issued white shirts to cover the sweat marks! I have seen it done on a few occasions and those individuals often end up finding a can of deodorant spray waiting for them in their correspondence tray or on the seat of their patrol car. I wonder what those officers use with some of the current black polo issued shirts? I guess that as the shirt is black they probably think it will hide the marks ... but definitely not the smell!

Back to you with your oversized kit bag groaning with boots, hats and all other items of your issued uniform as you enter the doors of your first police station. You will hopefully be met at the front counter or in the foyer by one of your tutors or mentors, who will take you inside and show you where you can put your bag. You will then change into your uniform in one of the locker rooms before being taken to meet the senior officer who is in charge of your policing area. There will be the usual 'welcome to the area' chat and maybe a few questions about you and what your career plans or ambitions may be after your initial training. The senior officer is likely to outline their expectations and explain what the biggest crime problems in the area are before wishing you luck and reassuring you that their door is always open if you have any problems. Best of luck with a) finding their door open or b) receiving a sympathetic hearing to a problem you may face. Whilst support within the force has widely improved, the open-door offer is generally just lip-service. The senior officer makes the offer but they don't expect every new recruit to pop in with any problems they face. Most problems are usually dealt with and supported by officers lower down the command chain. Smile and nod in the right places and, if you get that right, you should be out of there in fifteen minutes and handed back to a police sergeant. Sergeants are the backbone of the police service and carry out most of the general tasks, supervisory matters and overall running of every police station. The decisions may be made higher up the ranks, but delivering them and ensuring they are carried out falls to the police sergeant.

The sergeant will hopefully help you locate your locker and, if you are lucky, it will have a functioning locking mechanism. You may wonder why on earth you need a locking mechanism in a police station, of all places. After all, police officers are highly trained professionals who care for the public and protect society from all kinds of wrongdoing. But they are also forgetful souls who consider most issued uniform as collective property. At almost every football match or Public Order event, someone loses or forgets an item of uniform and hunts around the locker room for something they can 'borrow'. I worked on one event where one officer 'borrowed' a hat and another officer then 'borrowed' another hat, as he found that his had gone missing from on top of his locker. I did laugh when we sat down in the carrier and, as the hats came off, they both realised they were wearing the other's hat! Then there is the 'Tipp-Ex' person to contend with who will search for a decent deodorant or aftershave. I always had a simple answer to these problems in the locker room: I never left anything in my locker I didn't mind losing or sharing, and I only ever borrowed from people I knew. Hence most aftershave or deodorant you find, particularly in the men's locker room, will be of the Lynx or maybe Brut variety, the sort of aftershave you receive when you reach a certain age as a Christmas giftset. Rest assured, you can always 'borrow' the complimentary talcum powder or face scrub left behind by every locker owner from an old giftset. I have no idea if the ladies' locker rooms operate by the same sharing system. Judging by the conversations I overheard and some conversations I wished I hadn't, they share much more than the blokes do, and some also use the Tip-Ex method!

Having stored your kit away and now resplendent in your freshly pressed uniform, you will re-join the sergeant and your tutors/mentors for a longer introduction chat where they will explain what they expect from you. The best bit of advice I received as a very young police officer at training school about how to deal with my first few weeks at a police station was from a wise instructor. He told our class to 'Keep your eyes and ears open and your mouths shut.' The problem some new probationary police officers find is that they have a lot of theoretical knowledge and think they know exactly how to apply it. In real life, sometimes the theory needs to be adapted to deal with fast-changing situations and a more practical policing approach must be applied. Another piece of good advice is to always keep an open mind as opposed to telling other officers what the guidelines or study notes say they need to do.

After all the chats and completing any paperwork that is needed, you will walk out of the police station and onto the streets. You will inevitably do the 'shop window' walk, as you walk along the street for the very first time and glance and admire your reflection in the shop windows. The next thing you will become aware of is the reaction from the public as you walk along, and you start to notice the looks you are getting. People seem to be staring at you, or maybe they are avoiding eye contact. Some are even nodding or saying 'Hello' to you and you start to wonder if you know all these people, until you realise that it is what you represent that is attracting this response. It can be quite strange those first few months out on foot patrol or driving around as you start to notice the public's reaction to a uniformed police officer or vehicle. Drivers will inevitably slow down or start to indicate every small turn or deviation. Their hands go onto the steering wheel so they can drive exactly as they were taught, and they mostly avoid eye contact as they are concentrating on their driving. Try to make eye contact with people and smile or nod when you are out walking. The majority of the public are supportive of the police service and will welcome friendly officers as they go about their own business.

From your first day on patrol, this is now about developing your training and applying all the theory and the practical tests you were assessed on during your initial training. You will have an experienced officer alongside you, but they will allow you to deal with enquiries or incidents on your own both so you gain confidence and so that they can assess you. The first two years of your policing career involves constant assessment. In every situation and at every incident you attend, you should expect this assessment to be taking place as the tutor constable watches how you perform as a police officer. The amount of information and practical knowledge you are expected to absorb during your probationary period is enormous. I am often asked when my training was finally complete and there was nothing left to learn, but I don't think you ever stop learning or developing in any policing role as, in the very least, legislation, policies and guidelines are constantly being changed or revised, and every single incident or call is different. You can report ten burglaries in a shift and, although the basic offence is the same, the victims will certainly be different and their needs will not be the same, so a different method must be applied for each one. One of the positive points about being a police officer is that no two days are the same; you will meet so many people from different walks of life and you never stop learning or experiencing new things.

Of course, you get to know the more prolific offenders and criminals in your area, as well as the people who need help from the police on a frequent basis. Every policing area has their regular callers. We had a regular caller when I was at Fulham police station, who I will call Mr S. Every weekend he would phone the police station and report that aliens were trying to take him. Despite the best efforts of the call handlers, we inevitably had to send our squad specially trained in all things extra-terrestrial to see him. This was one of those calls as sergeant I would try to avoid, not because I wouldn't or couldn't deal with it, but mainly because I didn't want to hear what my officers were telling him! He took to wearing a hat made out of tin foil and rumour had it that one time, he lined his walls and covered his furniture with the silver foil lining as he believed it stopped the extra-terrestrials in their tracks and his calls for assistance reduced slightly. I have no idea which one of my team came up with this very inventive solution to his particular problem, but it certainly helped and Mr S was very happy. Please don't think we just gave flippant answers and left him to it, as he was regularly referred to social services and he had his own case worker who was on first name terms with most officers. He was harmless enough and capable of looking after himself, but we were duty-bound to check he was OK. It is a constant theme of every training course I deliver that police officers must keep an open mind at every incident and with everyone you deal with, even if you have been at their address on many previous occasions. The moment you start pre-judging or deciding how you are going to deal with a person or the incident before you have fully investigated the facts will be when you miss something and make a serious professional error.

As a probationary police officer you will serve two years before you are confirmed in the role and rank, during which time you will need to take more exams and attend further training. The CKP course is not included, so the two-year probation period effectively starts from the first day at training school and the day you swear the oath of allegiance. This is not some bizarre secret ceremony, but a sworn statement taken in front of a magistrate where you confirm that you will dutifully serve as a police officer. It is worded like this:

> I, – of –, do solemnly and sincerely declare and affirm that I will well and truly serve the Queen in the office of constable with fairness, integrity, diligence and impartiality, upholding fundamental human rights and according equal respect to all people; and that I will, to the best of my power, cause the peace to be kept and preserved and prevent all offences against people and property; and that while I continue to hold the said office I will to the best of my skill and knowledge discharge all the duties thereof faithfully according to law.

So, from the first day of training to what will hopefully be a long policing career, all the theory you learnt in the initial course will be put to the test. The one thing that no training course can ever really prepare you for is the public and their behaviour. There is no real way of knowing what type of person you will meet from day to day. Your trainers will have given you realistic scenarios to deal with but you cannot fully replicate personal characteristics or reactions to situations.

Trust in your training as that will give you the foundation when deciding what you need to do. You must also be mindful of your own characteristics and ability to listen, and you need to summarise what you have been told, assess what you can see, be decisive and explain concisely what you intend to do. I have found that people react better when you behave humanely. I have seen too many officers becoming almost robotic when reciting their powers. You might be wearing a uniform, but try to retain some personality and empathy for whatever or whoever you are dealing with. Be yourself even though you are now wearing a police uniform.

I may have forgotten to mention a small part of day one, and that is the fact that you are likely to be placed on to your team's shift system. You could well be working early turn or late turn on that first day. The exact times differ across the UK but, predominantly, early turn starts at 6 a.m. and late turn at 2 p.m. so you could well have been at work for four hours before your initial meeting with your local senior officer. Make sure you have worked out your travel arrangements prior to your first day and, if you are driving, find out where you can park and don't expect the same number of spaces to be available at 1 p.m. as you may find at 5 a.m. Not all police stations have parking facilities on site for the officers that work there, so make sure you give yourself plenty of time. Most sensible new recruits I know carry out a dry-run so they are relaxed about it before their first day. If you have never worked at the unsociable hours involved in policing, then it is important you test your route to work as days and times can have different effects on your journey. At 5 a.m. most people are still in bed so cars are still parked from the night before, which may mean that there are fewer available parking spaces for when you arrive at work. Parking restrictions will not have started for the day so cars may be parked in bays which are permitted overnight but not during the day. You would not be the first police officer on day one to finish for the day and find their car clamped when they return to it. Consider all possibilities for your journey to work and consult public transport times, taking account of weekday and weekend differences.

The last thing you want to be doing on your very first day is finding out the train you thought you could get was the weekend timetable as that's when you did your practice run. Day one is an important day for you and it is all about being prepared and planning ahead, which is similar to the skills you will need in policing. Your training will have prepared you in many ways but it is up to you to apply your new-found abilities and ensure that you are at work at the right time, ready to enforce the law.

What other training can you expect during your first two years and will you just be stuck learning beats and walking the streets?

CHAPTER 9

THINGS NO ONE TELLS YOU

ABOUT POLICING

After the euphoric first day at what will be your new policing home for possibly the next two years, what comes next? You are likely to have met one of the senior officers for your policing area and some, if not all, of the officers you will be working with. You have hopefully found a functioning locker and stored away your issued police uniform and then will have gone home to tell your family and friends about your first day in your new policing role. This is a bit like regressing back in time to your first day at school, as parents and family are keen to know exactly what you did on your first operational day as a police officer.

When you excitedly report you met a senior police officer and put your uniform in a locker, they might look a bit blank. So next you tell them about how you were given access to the police computers at your station and you managed to log on and read the daily briefing. This doesn't seem to impress them, so maybe you tell them you were taken out in a police car for an hour or so and even walked along a few streets. Eventually someone may ask, 'What, so no robbers or burglars or car chases? You didn't solve any crimes or deal with a murder in your first hour?'

Policing is not quite as it seems on most police TV shows and even the reality police programmes have been edited and condensed to show the 'interesting' bits. There are many aspects of policing that are routine and there can be lengthy periods of inactivity. These quiet periods do seem to have reduced over the last few years, no doubt aided by the government budget cuts which mean that there are fewer front-line officers to meet the increasing demand for policing. Whilst you may spend your time chasing one urgent call to the next, that's not the case everywhere. Your experience on your first day may well be different and you could go out on patrol and be first on scene at a serious incident. Alternatively, you could patrol for the next two years and never get close to dealing with anything like that. Policing is just that sort of vocation. You never really know what is going to happen each time you arrive for work and you can go from relative inactivity to a full-scale serious incident in seconds. Just as an aside, the word 'quiet' is never used by any experienced police officers as that has always seemed to be the cue for all hell to break loose. On so many occasions whilst on patrol or in a control room, the moment someone utters the words 'Quiet today, isn't it?' the phones start to ring off the hook. The quickest way to upset your new police colleagues and create chaos at work is to go around saying how quiet the day is. If you do make this mistake, I suggest you duck as you are liable to have several items thrown at you for doing so. It is this unpredictability that seems to attract so many people to join the police and it is the very thing that helps maintain their desire to keep doing the job for as long as they do.

As I mentioned earlier, during your probationary period you will attend further instructional courses. This includes the annual OST days that focus on practising the various techniques and approved tactics. You will receive refresher training on using your handcuffs, batons, CS spray, open hand tactics and restraint techniques. OST is continually evolving and there are always different elements to practise. It is this repetition that establishes muscle memory, and this benefits officers when they are required to use force in a situation. Each session usually ends with one of the instructors in what is called a 'fist suit' as they play the part of a member of the public who confronts you. The 'fist suit' is essentially a full-body suit made of padded protective plates that protects the instructor's body when being struck. Think of the iconic Michelin Man and you'll get the idea. You will be given a brief scenario and then the instructor will confront you and you need to use reasonable force to deal with them. The reasonable force you use may include baton strikes if you have been given one of the foam-padded training batons, or maybe hand and leg strikes. It could even be resolved using just effective communication, even if you enter the room and are confronted with a knife- or baton-wielding 'suspect'. A key part of the training is learning that an officer's use of force is dictated by what the suspect does and not to escalate the incident straight away. It is very important to realise that many situations can be resolved with clear and effective communication, only using force when strictly necessary and reasonable. This scenario seems to last for ages because all your decisions and actions are carefully assessed, but it is usually only around a minute long. You must remember that each individual strike needs to be justified by you and each training session you attend emphasises just how important it is to validate every single action taken. You need to be reasonably fit to complete this aspect of police training, hence the annual fitness test and the compulsory warm up exercises before each training session. This forms part of your ongoing training assessment throughout your policing career and it applies equally to every officer, whatever their role or rank, including senior officers and detectives.

During your probationary period, you will attend further training days to receive additional inputs on offences and legislation that were not covered during your initial recruit training or on the CKP. Blackmail, abstracting electricity and some football related offences are just some pieces of legislation that are delivered during your two-year probationary period. You will also have to complete National Centre for Applied Learning Technologies (NCALT) packages whilst at work to keep up-to-date with legislation changes and revised policy guidelines. The NCALT method is much maligned and sometimes laborious. Whilst the computer-based training packages that facilitate learning online are very useful, it is considered poor training for operational police officers. It offers no interaction with a trainer or any opportunity to make any queries or points. It is a one-way delivery method with no flexibility for different learning styles or teaching methods, and many don't like it.

Clicking your way through the NCALT method however, does make it a cost-effective way to disseminate revised or new training packages about a variety of different subjects, including legislation and policing skills. You will log onto the system and read through the package, watch videos and, on some occasions, there are tests at the end to ensure understanding. The NCALT is a national system, so every police force uses it. Whether it is effective or provides the best training is debatable, but the alternative is to take officers off the streets and have them sit in classrooms for days at a time learning new and revised policing practices. That would inevitably attract additional costs for trainers and accommodation and would remove officers from operational policing for extended periods of time. Although it may not be perfect, in my opinion NCALT training does generally achieve its objective. Even so, whilst it delivers the required training package in a timely and cost-effective way and has been significantly improved over the last few years, NCALT should not fully replace the traditional classroom-based learning that allows healthy debate and discussion. Shared experiences and opinions will be of equal or greater benefit on many occasions to those learning than merely listening to an online instructor teach you the subject. The main issue with NCALT based training packages is that it makes it impossible to query the subject matter. There is significant scope for improvement in further training for the police, with the enhanced use of technology and programs such as webinar or live chat being potentially utilised. Some subjects are too important to be left to a non-responsive tutorial package.

In addition to the instructor-led days and the NCALT packages, you will undoubtedly receive guidance from experienced members of your team. Some of it will be explained patiently, but on other occasions your colleagues may be slightly blunter in their explanation and you will be left under no illusions what you need to do!

The best advice I would give to anybody is to watch and listen to how your colleagues deal with incidents and the public. There will be some methods that you like and there will be some you may have a different view on. Police officers are all human and, although they receive the same training, their personality and characteristics will remain to a great extent in their approach to people and incidents. The initial training will give you a template for the questions and actions that must be performed at incidents or investigations. You should try to remember the magnificent seven when asking questions: who, what, why, where, when, which and how. You will hear some of your experienced colleagues ask the same questions but maybe not with the same empathy you have been instructed to exercise. Whilst police training needs to be ordered and specific to ensure the required information is learnt, it is down to the individual to decide how they deliver the required questions or conduct the investigation. A general rule of thumb is to always treat everyone you encounter in your policing duties exactly how you would want your own family to be treated. That advice may alter slightly if the individual or group tries to cause you injury or harm, but you should always try to be approachable, reasonable and fair in your general dealings with public enquiries or allegations of crime. Remember, people will be able to recount any dealings with the police for years to come, so never underestimate how great an impression you can have.

The real challenge when you first start as a police officer is to observe without starting to offer guidance to more experienced colleagues about how to do their jobs. That doesn't mean to say you cannot ask questions about what they have done and why. You just have to remember that although police training is conducted in a certain way to ensure police officers know their responsibilities, on occasions practicalities may mean the method must be adapted to fit the incident and people involved. I have previously said that you never stop learning as a police officer and there are always new guidelines or methods to adapt to. The balance you must find as a new police officer is to be naturally inquisitive without criticising your colleagues' style or method. The training staff will advise you as to how and when you should challenge inappropriate or unprofessional behaviour and it is vitally important you do so, as any bad behaviour can undermine the work of all officers. As I mentioned at the start, take the best from every person you work with and leave behind anything else you do not like. You will find your own methods and the initial training and instruction you receive provides a good foundation for you to do that.

As a probationary police officer, you will be given some mundane tasks such as standing guard on a prisoner in hospital or remaining at a crime scene cordon for many hours. This really is all part of the learning process and essential working experience every officer should go through to fully understand the demands of the job. If one day you reach the heights of being a senior investigating officer, you will appreciate more fully what the officers standing by the police tape are doing and the importance of their role in the investigation. The best senior officers I worked with and for were the ones who had experienced all the menial tasks in the early days of their careers. They understood exactly what they were asking to be done on their behalf, as they had personally experienced it and had not just read about it in an instruction manual or seen it in a classroom.

One of the most formative days of my early career was on New Year's Day in 1981. At the time, I was living in the police section house at the back of the police station in Tooting, and the New Year's Eve party was in the downstairs gym. I knew I was on early turn the next day with a 6 a.m. start and that I would also be working as the station telephonist that day. The civilian telephonists did not work bank holidays so we needed a police officer to work the old-fashioned switchboard. This was one of the mundane tasks I had already performed many times before as a new probationer. The switchboard was the type you see in black and white films with numerous cords and corresponding holes for each extension and, when it was busy, it resembled a plate of spaghetti. There were approximately five or six lines into the police station and you had two rows of cords in front of you. You answered all incoming calls with the rear cord by placing the plug into the flashing socket and then, once you established who the caller wanted, you placed the front cord nearest you into the corresponding slot on the main board. This may sound easy, but many of my colleagues found it hard work and frequently disconnected the commander or chief superintendent by pulling out more than one cord and connecting a caller to the wrong extension.

I was confident that on New Year's Day from 6 a.m. to 2 p.m. there would not be too many senior police officers in the building, and so the switchboard would not be that challenging. I could sit with my feet up and put the audible alarm on so I would see and hear any calls and then I could just relax and enjoy earning my double-time. I decided to thoroughly participate in the party and drank a fair amount of alcohol, knowing I could comfortably sleep it off in the telephonist's room for eight hours. I went another step further by deciding to stay up and party all night and forego any sleep. Well, it was New Year's Eve and I knew I was just going to be sitting down all day and answering a few phone calls – how hard could that be?

I eventually went off to my room at about 5.30 a.m. to put on my uniform in preparation for my telephonist's stint.

I wandered into the front office at Tooting police station at about 5.50 a.m., having showered and shaved in a fairly half-hearted attempt to appear awake and ready for the day, but already anticipating a couple of hours snoozing on the switchboard. I opened the door to the telephonist's room and nearly fell over in shock as I saw Shirley, one of our telephonists, sitting in her chair! 'Morning, love! It's OK, I decided to come in today so you are not needed.' As lovely as it was to see Shirley I now had a dilemma, as I wanted the double-time payment for work-ing a bank holiday, but the couple of pints (!) I had drunk and the lack of sleep was a problem. I found my sergeant, aptly (and not-so-sympathetically) nicknamed 'Ticker' due to the fact he had a heart scare a few years previously. I learnt that day if you ever want sympathy, do not ask any of your colleagues: they are great at being sympathetic with the public, but completely the opposite when it comes to officers!

I explained that my telephonist role had been filled and asked Ticker what I should do instead. I was really hoping he would find me something easy to do that might involve sitting in a car and grabbing some sleep, although at that point I would have accepted being told I wasn't needed. As it happened, the front window of the shoe-shop 'Ravels' in Tooting High Street had been smashed overnight and the premises were insecure. One of my night-duty colleagues was standing on it to prevent the shop being further damaged or any stock being stolen and

I was sent to go and take over. My sergeant had found me something worthwhile to do and assured me I could stay on duty for the much sought-after double-time payment, so all was starting to look up. The problem was, however, that the key holder lived in north London and was coming in on public transport. Remember, this was a bank holiday in 1981 and the Northern line was not due to start running until much later that morning. One of the night-duty cars drove me straight down to the shop so their own colleague could get off to bed. By 6 a.m., I found myself with my raincoat and helmet on standing on the pavement outside a broken window rather than sleeping on the switchboard. This was not part of my master plan! I now regretted staying up all night and drinking the second (or fourth) pint and those vodkas hadn't helped me either. By 8 a.m. I had not seen a single soul walk past the shop (no pun!) and had become quite bored of:

1. Counting the shoes
2. Counting the roof tiles
3. Counting the men's shoes
4. Counting the ladies' shoes
5. Finally, stepping into the shop window and pretending to be a mannequin. I obviously pioneered the mannequin challenge that is now so popular – I was clearly way ahead of my time!

I decided that my best plan was to grab some shut-eye, so I bundled up my raincoat to use it as a pillow and clambered into the shop window. I decided the best place to lie down was amongst the high heel boots and ladies' shoes – no idea why, but it was quite pleasant. I was woken a short time later with a start when I heard the two-tone horns of a police car and sat up to see our area car parked on the pavement and right alongside my new bedroom. Once the driver and radio operator had both stopped laughing, a steaming cup of hot tea emerged from the driver's window and it tasted better than anything I had consumed in years. They told me the key-holder was on their way and should be with me by 10 a.m. They even handed me a bacon roll. After some healthy mickey-taking about my choice of sleeping accommodation including some uncalled for references about me in high-heeled boots, off they went and promised to come back and collect me when the key-holder turned up.

My natural body clock kicked in and when the shop owner arrived, I looked thoroughly professional and the shoes were back on their stand. He was extremely happy that we had secured the premises from any further loss overnight and was astonished we had stood guard for the whole time. I obviously accepted all the praise and somehow forgot to mention I had only been there for four hours and a colleague had had the longer and more boring stint. After I had written down the details required for the crime report, my promised lift duly returned to whisk me back to the warm confines of our canteen. I wrote a crime report so lengthy and detailed that Hercule Poirot or Sherlock Holmes would have been proud. It took me a good couple of hours to fully complete as I managed to slowly thaw out in the warmth of the police canteen and allow the effects of the vodka and beer to disappear.

The main point here is that my colleagues in the area car fully understood the onerous task I had been given, hence their visit to me armed with tea and a bacon roll. I tried to do the same throughout my career for any colleagues given similar duties to perform because I knew exactly what it was like, having experienced it myself. Here's a helpful tip for anyone: never ask anyone to do something you are not prepared to do or have done yourself. It is a huge part of gaining respect from your colleagues and why during your probationary two-year period you will be asked to do all manner of mundane policing tasks to form part of your overall learning.

Another important thing to understand is that having a sense of humour and maintaining balance in your own life is another challenge you will face when learning how to be a police officer. Different people cope in various ways with the stress and anxiety of the job. Humour is frequently used to help alleviate stress, although it may seem slightly inappropriate to the uninitiated eye. As I mentioned earlier, in my first five years as a police officer I dealt with four suicides where death was caused by hanging, as well as one suicide where the individual set themselves on fire and at least two fatal accidents. The day after one of the fatal accidents, I had to take the fingerprints of the deceased in the mortuary to identify him. You will have to develop your own way to cope with the impact this type of work will have. Some may well criticise the banter and maybe even consider it to be bullying. I do not subscribe to that opinion as I think laughter and humour can help people cope, provided it is not unjust or cruel. Being able to laugh at yourself is extremely important and you may even acquire the odd nickname during your police service. I had several, including 'wet one' (due to my surname) and 'wiggy', which I gained on account of the thickness of my head of hair which, in the early days, did resemble a wig. To this day many of my former colleagues still refer to me as 'wiggy' and I am even saved in some mobile phones under that name! A good and balanced sense of humour will support you through the challenging times of being a police officer and laughing at yourself with your colleagues will often relieve stressful situations.

The important aspect to remember here, however, is the impression you make on the public and anyone else you are dealing with at a particular incident. Professionalism must be maintained at all times, but that does not stop the odd wind-up taking place every now and then. There was a phase early in my career where we would hide our colleagues' lockers in strange places around the police station. One ended up on the canteen roof and its owner happily changed up there for a week or so until the guilty culprits returned it to the locker room … sorry Kevin! He did get his revenge a few weeks later. Our area car driver Barry opened his front door to leave his house at 5.15 a.m. for an early turn and walked straight into his own locker in his front porch! To this day, he cannot work out how we unlocked the porch door and placed it there, and all before 5.15 a.m. Barry arrived at work with the rear hatch of his two-door sports car open and his locker sticking out of the back. The jokes have been modernised to a certain extent, and these days they seem to revolve around phones and social media. You do need to take care with anything placed on public forums, as that is where the joke can be widely viewed and it may affect the reputation of the police service. By all means, banter amongst your colleagues is fine and it even helps to defuse the stress of the job. Just be careful when it comes to anything that could cause a serious problem for the police service and all those involved.

There are two distinct roles, either as a community or neighbourhood police officer or on the response teams dealing with the 999 emergency calls. Both are essential in providing an effective and balanced police service. The public like to see officers in the community but they also want the reassurance that police officers will be there when they have an emergency. You could well move between both roles during your first two years so that you have the knowledge and experience of a community police officer and the exposure in dealing with emergency calls as part of a response team.

You may have the opportunity to move to a different role and I know of some former students who have moved to a detective role before the end of their two-year probation. I will deal with the role of the Criminal Investigation Department (CID) later, but the other much sought-after role is driving. A very frequent question on every police recruit training course is 'When will I be able to drive a police car and what is the training like?'

CHAPTER 10

I WANT TO DRIVE POLICE CARS

A very popular question on any course I have been involved with is always about when the recruits can start driving with blue lights on. The majority of people, it would appear, want to drive a police car with the sirens on and lights flashing and swerve in and out of traffic. It is an added bonus when you are doing this if you have a getaway car in front of you in a scene reminiscent of so many Hollywood films. The prevalence of the iconic car chase seems to have been a mainstay of so many films in recent years. I am not sure what the attraction is for many of us to be able to speed through the streets with lights flashing and sirens wailing like some latter-day knight in shining armour racing to the rescue of someone. For me, as I've mentioned before, the TV series *The Sweeney* was a key part of wanting to be a police officer. Most episodes involved a scene with their unmarked cars racing to the scene of a crime or chasing bank robbers or the like, ending in a spectacular car crash.

The bloke driving the car in *The Sweeney* was my role model. Sitting quietly in the background but always being ready to speed through the streets with effortless skill and calm ability. I fancied some of that and had decided by the time I joined in September 1979 that I wanted to drive police cars and, more importantly, I wanted to be an advanced driver. It is important at this point to recognise that not every police force has the same application process, waiting time or criteria for those wanting to become a police driver. I cannot tell you exactly how to apply to be a police driver as the procedure differs greatly from force to force, but I will take you through the general process and describe my own experience. What is a consistent fact is that the police service has different categories or grades of drivers, although each force might have different names or titles depending on where you are a serving officer. I can speak from experience about London and the Metropolitan Police as I was a Class 1 advanced driver and driving assessor when I was a police officer. The Met and many other forces essentially have three categories of driver and, in order of sequence, they are basic, standard/response and advanced. Regardless of how long you have held a driving licence, you will need to undergo some assessment first. As far as I have found, there are no police forces that will teach you to drive from the beginning, so you must have passed the normal driving test before you can even think of applying to become a police driver.

As ever, we may as well start at the beginning. Every police officer will have to pass a check test or driving assessment to become a basic police driver. I used to organise and supervise these training days in the Hammersmith and Fulham Borough in London and they are not challenging at all. The time that you can take this test largely depends on your force policy and whether they train all their officers to be police drivers during their initial training. The national guidelines are set by the College of Policing and they state the following about basic police drivers:

- It is the first step of their police driving career
- It requires a relevant induction package commensurate with their role and organisation procedures but no necessity for on-road driving assessments
- They are required to meet the standard expected of a careful and competent driver within the law
- They are able to meet driving at work requirements
- They must only drive within the constraints of the Highway Code

- They are not permitted to drive any police vehicle in a situation that might involve the use of legal exemptions – use of legal exemptions requires appropriate driver training

Even after three classifications and some intensive courses, you must still abide by the road traffic law and will be driving using your own driving licence, since there is not a separate police driving licence. Police officers may receive certain exemptions for give-way lines and speeding amongst others, but only if it is safe, necessary and justified in the circumstances. If a collision occurs then you may be prosecuted and receive points on your personal driving licence. This could also affect your personal car insurance. In essence, you do not receive a separate licence to drive police vehicles so, although you are on duty and driving in response-mode or answering urgent calls, the licence you are using is your own personal one. There have been calls recently for a separate driving licence for emergency work purposes but, to date, these have been declined. I would fully support such a licence as the fire engine driver and police officer do not drive their own car in the same way they are called upon to drive their work vehicles.

So basic police drivers must follow the Highway Code and drive according to the law. They are not permitted to drive using blue lights or sirens and cannot get away with any of the legal exemptions that may be granted to a trained police driver.

This means no exceeding the speed limit or going through red traffic lights as a basic driver. To explain the basic driving test, I will describe the days I used to run as a driving assessor. Firstly, you will be told when you can apply to become a basic driver if it is not part of your initial training. Usually, this is when your unit needs more people trained and places are normally allocated to the longest serving officers not yet trained to drive police vehicles. When you attend the training day, you have to take a theory test which is very similar to the public Highway Code exam, and you must pass this. Next, there may be some classroom-based instruction about the expectations of a police driver and a reminder to adhere to the Highway Code at all times. In essence, you are expected to drive competently and carefully. There will also be some guidance provided about how to book the vehicles out for use and how to conduct a check to make sure the vehicle is legal and roadworthy. In London, you also have to complete a practical driving assessment on the public roads.

This has changed since basic drivers were first introduced in the late '80s. My usual on-road assessment in those days for any prospective basic driver involved getting them to drive me to Burger King on a Sunday late turn. If we managed to return to the police station with the buns intact with the burgers, the milkshakes in one piece with the lids still on and the chips located in their containers, they passed. Many of my team became basic drivers by virtue of this simple yet effective test to see how carefully they could drive. This whole process became standardised in the late '90s and I attended my official driving assessor's course for supervisors in 1999.

As a sergeant and a Class 1 driver, I could apply for the course and then run my own basic driving days. On the basic test days you sit a theory test, which is usually a multiple-choice exam and marked whilst you wait, before you go out for an assessed drive if you have passed the theory test. All that the assessor wants in that practical drive is for you to show you can control the car competently and considerately within the Highway Code. I used to say to those about to take the driving assessment to imagine they were taking their mum to the shops. We were not looking for a scary police car chase during the basic test. In truth, that was the last thing we wanted and it would have been an automatic fail. Everyone usually passed this test as they were already full licence holders and were very used to driving. On one occasion Steve, a young probationer who had never driven a car before in London, asked me if he could do the test. I had some concerns, but after some pressure from his colleagues on my team, I agreed he could do the test and I would arrange an assessment day just for him and take him out for the drive. A highly educated young man, he sailed through the theory test, and then we ventured to the streets of Fulham. We had an audience as I ran him through how to check police vehicles every time we come on duty to make sure they are roadworthy. This process is called the daily inspection, or DI for short, and you check everything from the tyres, including the tread and pressures, to lights, indicators and the horn. I then ran him through what is known as the 'cockpit drill', where you sit in the driver's seat and talk your way through the instrument panel and controls to ensure you are familiar with the vehicle's operations and features. Having completed the checks we slowly, very slowly, drove out the station gates.

Off we went for a very short basic assessment drive that usually lasts around fifteen to twenty minutes. We turned left onto the very busy North End Road. I could see Steve was now realising that this was not as easy as it had sounded in the canteen with his colleagues egging him on. As his confidence grew, he sped up and started to match our speed with the traffic and we even overtook one lady with a walking frame. I took him on a circuitous route around Fulham and we eventually wound our way into Munster Road, having turned left at Fulham Cross to go back towards the police station. Munster Road is a busy main road that runs parallel to Fulham Palace Road and is used as a popular cut-through, so the local authority has installed road humps along the length of it to deter many from this short cut. There are several shops and cars parked on both sides of the road so it is narrowed and difficult to deal with oncoming traffic. I began to regret my decision instantly as Steve steered the car towards the passenger side every time a car came towards us. We had one or two close shaves with parked cars with just a Rizla paper's measure of distance between wing mirrors! It was almost inevitable that when the next car came towards us, over to the left we went and we heard a 'thud' as our wing mirror clipped a parked car. I told him to pull over as I needed to get out and check the damage, but astonishingly the lucky little bugger had caused no damage whatsoever, not even a scuff mark. I then inspected our police vehicle and lightning does strike twice, because that was also undamaged with not a single mark on the wing mirror. This was probably due to the fact that we were driving so slowly that it was just a very light contact.

We drove back into the police station with Steve sitting next to me with a very glum look on his face. Our colleagues from our response team were all waiting and burst into fits of laughter when they saw me at the wheel. I quickly jumped out of the vehicle and left him to explain our journey, having told him to go out and practise driving in London before asking to do this again. Luckily, this little setback did him no harm at all as I believe he is now a chief inspector and running his own unit. I just hope he has his own driver!

Hopefully, your basic driving assessment will be less fraught and you will pass the theory test and practical assessment with no trouble. You will then be able to drive a police vehicle in a non-response mode. But what is the next step to progress and drive with sirens on and lights flashing?

Standard or response driving is the next stage and this covers the majority of police drivers. This step may take a bit longer to complete and, again, it depends on where you work and the need for drivers. It is usually offered to officers once they have completed their two-year probationary period but there may be some forces and officers who complete this course before finishing their probation. I was lucky enough to go on my standard car driving course in June 1981 just a few months short of completing my two-year probation.

I had been a police cadet and joined at eighteen-and-a-half, as many cadets did. When I was posted to my team in Tooting, I met up with another former cadet who was about six months ahead of me and also living in the section house. Chris was on my team so we used to patrol together occasionally and, after a few months, he announced that he was sitting his driving test to prepare himself for the next available driving course. I already had my full licence but, as I mentioned, course allocation largely fell to seniority and he was six months ahead of me in police service, so he was next in line for a spot on the course. After he proudly announced he had passed his driving test, he bought the most awful bright yellow Renault 21 and insisted on driving this mobile 'sunbeam' everywhere to get the practice. A few months passed and after he completed his probation around May he was duly assigned to a driving course. We all wished him luck as off he went to start his course at the world-famous Hendon Police Driving School. Later that afternoon, I was urgently called back to the station to see my inspector and the duties sergeant. As I nervously entered the station, I was met by one of my sergeants who quickly whispered to me it was about a driving course and I was not in the shit!

I knocked on the duty inspector's office door and my team inspector, John, shouted 'Come in!' in his easily recognisable Scottish accent. He told me that there was a space on the standard car driving course if I wanted it and if I could get to Hendon the next day. I nearly jumped up and kissed him before excitedly accepting without a second thought for any plans I might have had over the next three weeks. It was only after we had checked for any prior commitments that I considered asking about Chris and whether I was on the course with him. John explained that there had been a problem with Chris and it was his place I was taking, but he could not tell me any more at that stage. I left the office delighted at my own piece of good luck but more than slightly curious as to what problems had arisen for Chris. Having confirmed my availability and attendance, off I dashed to the canteen to tell my team, who were already up-to-date on Chris losing his driving course to me.

The station was full of speculation that evening as we all pondered what could have happened with Chris but, as ever in policing, there was inevitably someone who could find out. Remember, police officers are a very tight-knit group and it's usually easy to find someone in-the-know. One of our team knew someone at the driving school and, a few phone calls later, we found out that Chris had turned up ready for his driving course, but failed to overcome the very first hurdle. On every driving course, you have to produce your driving licence. Astonishingly, Chris had not passed his driving test when he told us that he had and had been driving around without L plates unsupervised and therefore without any car insurance, as his policy was set up for a learner driver. Apparently, he initially claimed to have forgotten his licence and then produced it, hoping it would not be examined thoroughly! I could not believe he could be this naive, especially at the driving school where most of the instructors were all former traffic officers.

In light of Chris's bad luck, I went on the course and passed. I never actually saw Chris again as by the time I returned to Tooting, he had resigned from the police and was being prosecuted for the driving offences. I could not believe that to save-face with his colleagues he would start a lie about passing a driving test and then actually try to bluff his way through a driving course. I have no idea why he didn't just decline the course and then quietly pass his test at some future date, although that would mean that he'd have still been committing driving offences. A sad end to a friend's career but an important lesson learnt about honesty and openness. It was a real shame as he showed great promise as a police officer, but clearly had made an awful error in judgement and then paid a very high price.

You may have to wait a bit longer than I did and hopefully there will be no repeat of the circumstances which led to me getting my standard driving classification. The standard/response course is usually around three weeks long and you will be taught how to drive according to the police drivers' manual, or *Roadcraft* as it is called. This book is available for anyone to buy and if you are serious not only about becoming a police officer but also about being a police driver, then it is an absolute must-have for you to read. It takes you through the system of car control, which is 'a system or drill each feature of which is considered in sequence by the driver on the approach to any hazard'. I promise I did not have to look that up as I can still remember it from my driving courses over thirty years ago! *Roadcraft* also teaches you how to use the blue lights and sirens. You will practise blue-light runs on public roads with an experienced instructor alongside you in a marked police vehicle. The vehicles are not dual control and neither are they improved or enhanced in any way, something which debunks another popular myth. Police cars are standard road cars with some livery markings and emergency lights added – and nothing else! No souped-up engines or performance enhancements, just highly trained drivers. This course is your first introduction to the official method of police driving and the College of Policing guidelines have the following to say about the standard/response course.

A standard/response driver:

- Must have a category B/A DVLA licence as a prerequisite
- Is permitted to drive low to intermediate performance vehicles
- Is not expected to use unmarked police vehicles to 'respond' in a pursuit situation – if this is permitted by a force, an appropriate risk assessment must be in place and a suitable level of training provided commensurate with operational requirements.

Emphasis is placed on safety, achieved by the driver having an increased general awareness of the vehicle's handling and performance, as well as the ability to recognise real and potential hazards.

The course itself is all about being safe and aware of other road users. Once you pass your standard/response course, you can start to answer emergency calls and use your blue lights and sirens to facilitate your progress through traffic. You can exceed the speed limit and treat red lights as give way signs, provided it is safe to do so. The overriding factor is always safety for you and all other road users. Remember, no call is so urgent as to justify an accident. Safety is a constant focus of the course and you will have to justify every manoeuvre or use of excess speed. It is a difficult course both physically and mentally, as you are driving for long periods with an instructor and two other students watching your every move. You alternate so there is about an hour of actual driving for each student in the morning and then another hour each in the afternoon; but trust me, you are still concentrating and watching everything the other drivers do even when it's their turn. Although it's difficult, it remains a thoroughly enjoyable and worthwhile course and it does wonders to significantly raise your own driving ability – and you may even receive a discount on personal car insurance as well!

I can still remember my first ever day driving a marked police car after passing my standard driving course. We were on early turn at Tooting Police Station and I was posted to the panda car, as they were known. It was a two-door Ford Escort Mark 2 in that very pale blue colour with white door panels. I religiously carried out my daily inspection and all but got a magnifying glass out as I checked it thoroughly for any existing damage. I drove out of the yard and spent about an hour or so driving around the area, as for some strange reason it was quite exhilarating to drive around the foot patrol beats I had become so used to but was now able to cover in far less time. When I returned to the station, I turned right into the marked parking bay which was facing the red-brick wall. I drove slowly in and was trying to gauge the distance between my front bumper and the wall when there was a loud 'thump'. Bugger, or maybe something stronger, went through my mind. My first day out and I drive the panda car into the wall at the station! I got out of the car after reversing it slightly and examined the damage. Police regulations are quite strict when it comes to reporting any damage to vehicles, and each police vehicle has its own specific log book which contains a section for any minor damage to be recorded with a diagram of the vehicle. This section must only be completed by the reporting officer and that is usually a traffic supervisor or, more commonly called, the garage sergeant. The panda I had driven was a very old 'S' registration and there were already several imperfections across its bodywork. I spent ages looking and feeling with my fingertips, but there wasn't a single new scratch or dent. Although regulations are strict, there has to be some damage to require it to be reported. Since I could find nothing at all, it was a very lucky escape for me and one I kept to myself!

You could remain a standard/response driver for the rest of your career and never take another driving course again, although there will be refresher training and check tests whilst you remain an operational police driver. It is important that your driving standards and ability are periodically reviewed to make sure you still drive to the 'system of car control' and the guidelines of *Roadcraft*.

In London, they have recently added the initial phases of pursuit training to the standard/response course, but this aspect of their driver training is limited. In reality, response cars form the bulk of police emergency response vehicles so it is understandable that most pursuits are usually initiated by response drivers as there are more of them and they are usually first on scene. There needed to be some initial training given to response drivers in how to risk assess and commence a vehicle pursuit and then ask for assistance from a fully authorised and trained pursuit driver.

The next step is the advanced driving course, and this also usually takes around three weeks to complete. It is designed to develop the driver's skills and ability from the response course and it also includes pursuit training as a specialised skill together with other specialised driving roles. The College of Policing guidance has this to say about the advanced driver training: 'The focus for advanced police driving/riding is to develop existing competencies and skills to a higher level than that expected in the standard/response module. Advanced drivers/riders are predominantly deployed in a road's policing patrol vehicle, an armed response vehicle or unmarked police vehicles used by surveillance officers.'

The current course format in London requires students to spend the first week in unmarked automatic vehicles to review and refresh their understanding of car control. The second week uses the traditional and trusted two-car follow method. This is where you drive out in two unmarked cars, one lead car and one follow car, and you follow each other around the public roads. This allows each of the three students in the car to become accustomed to watching a vehicle they are following and to drive accordingly. This is done whilst still applying the *Roadcraft* principles to your driving and using the system of car control and assessing any actual or potential risks. After a couple of days of this, students will progress to driving unmarked vehicles with two tones and blue lights on main roads, dual carriageways and motorways. They will also practise convoy driving, which is where you follow a lead vehicle and ensure the whole convoy can make every turn and exit together. The vehicles are usually positioned slightly off-set behind each other, so each driver has a view of the road ahead.

The final week steps up the training and combines all aspects of the first two weeks. There is a night drive to ensure that students are competent with driving in the dark with all the added risks of reduced visibility. Students will drive marked cars using blue lights and two tones and there will be several days of pursuit training. There is always a 'final drive' which is a pass/fail test and this is usually taken in the middle or towards the end of the third week. In this, the student drives a marked police vehicle with blue lights and sirens and pursues one of the instructors, who will be driving an unmarked vehicle. All of this training is conducted on public roads at normal times with other road users with a huge emphasis on safety, so that it effectively replicates real-life situations. There are some aspects of the training course that have not changed much from my advanced course in 1985, such as the two-car follow method and the night drive and pursuit training. If you successfully pass, you become an advanced driver and will most definitely receive discounts on your car insurance, although that only seems to apply whilst you are a serving officer as I discovered when I retired! As was the case with my standard/response course, I was once again very fortunate to be in the right place at the right time when I was allocated to an advanced driving course.

I had recently transferred to Merton Borough in March 1985 as the Met Police had started a policy where every officer would be compulsory transferred at five-year intervals throughout their service. This policy applied to every officer or so it was alleged, although I knew of some who mysteriously managed to evade being moved and the cynic in me suspected it was because they were part of some secret club. This compulsory transfer scheme was a stupid and nonsensical management decision put in place without any reasonable justification, but it stayed in place for a couple of years. I was duly moved a mile or two down the road to Mitcham police station to 'develop my policing career'. At the time I had passed my van driving course, which in those days was the course between the standard and the advanced courses. The van course lasted only three days or so and it involved being taught the towing method and learning to drive and reverse just using wing mirrors.

Within a few months of my arrival at Mitcham there were rumours circulating about a couple of advanced driving courses coming to the division, and all the eligible officers started to 'drop in' to the duties office with biscuits and other enticements. The system back then was that the duties office decided which shift, or relief, as they were called, would take the driving course. The supervisors would hold a discussion and nominate an eligible candidate from their officers to go on the course. We had two advanced drivers out of fifteen officers at Mitcham on my particular relief and two at Wimbledon on our corresponding relief. I didn't think we stood a chance, but the course was somehow allocated to Andy, a good friend of mine on our team. He was due to start the course in June as I was just starting my three-month posting on a divisional support unit (DSU), who were the forerunner of what is now the Territorial Support Group (TSG) and covered the gap after the Special Patrol Group (SPG) were disbanded. Prior to starting any advanced course, you had to take a check test with an assessor, which is still the case today. Andy went up to take his check test on the Monday before he was due to start his course and inexplicably failed it. Luckily for me, I happened to be working in the police station where the assessor was based. My phone went on the Tuesday morning at my home and it was our not-so-friendly duties sergeant. I was due to be working a 4 p.m. to midnight shift that day but he said 'If you can get your arse to Surbiton and see PS Palmer in the next couple of hours and pass, you are on the course starting next Monday.' I arranged my check test within the next hour and off I went and, luckily, I was living just a ten-minute drive from Surbiton. I passed the check test which entailed a twenty-minute drive along the A3 dual carriageway – virtually around the area where I was living!

The following Monday found me at Hendon Driving School just four years after passing my standard car course. I had to cram for the theory test yet again as that is taken on the first morning and I had just four days to prepare for the course as opposed to everyone else who had at least two weeks. The course in those days was six weeks long with phase one lasting two weeks and the second phase covering the remainder. Every day Monday to Friday, I travelled up to Hendon from Tolworth in Surrey by driving to Morden tube station at 6 a.m. and staying on the Northern line through twenty-seven stations. The course was tough and very demanding, but I managed to pass it as a Class 1 driver. The classification was dictated solely by your final drive mark and 75–84 per cent was a Class 2 and 86 percent upwards was a Class 1 – no 85 per cent marks were ever awarded for some reason! I had the chief instructor for my final drive and managed to attain an 87 per cent from him which I was told was almost unheard of. One of my instructors sat in the back of my car for my final drive as he was learning to be an assessor and he told me he would have given me 90 per cent, but I managed to flick the wipers on once instead of the indicators and that cost me one mark, equivalent to 3 per cent! The final drives are still just as tough and harshly marked.

Once again, I had been lucky enough to be ready and available for a short notice course and I returned to Mitcham as a Class 1 driver on a Monday morning for my first early turn shift. I can remember walking into the station on the following Monday morning feeling like I had won the lottery. After six weeks of intensive training, I was as good as I was ever going to be and so I expected to be allocated to at least one of the driving posts. Our sergeant was a wily old character who knew how to deal with this sort of 'Billy big bollocks' behaviour and I learnt a valuable lesson that morning. He ran through the postings and there was already a crew on our area car that were just finishing their month's posting, and the driver was unlikely to relinquish that for me … I wouldn't have, either! He ran through the three panda cars and the van but didn't mention my shoulder number, and I could see my colleagues looking at me and wondering what my posting was. I thought he hadn't realised I was in the room so when he finished the postings, I decided to speak up. 'Morning, Sarge, back from my advanced course and wondered what you would like me to drive today?' Sergeant Barry looked up from his postings sheet and peered over his glasses that were perched on the end of his nose. A wry smile started to spread across his face which was worrying at the best of times and almost terrifying at 6 a.m., and I immediately regretted speaking up. He looked down again at his list and said, 'Ah, 490, yes, here you are right at the bottom of my list.' This was getting far worse … bottom of the list meant only one thing and here it came. An undisguised element of delight was in his voice as he said 'Welcome back from your advanced driving course and as a Class 1 driver as well. You are five-beat today, refs at 10 a.m. and can you cover the school crossing patrol this morning and at lunchtime.' I did not need to look around the room as I could hear the sniggers from my colleagues who found this highly amusing. I had returned like some hero from the highest classification driving course in the Met and I was now consigned to walking round with a big hat on and ushering primary school children across the road. I had an audience as I walked out onto the streets and, funnily enough, almost every panda car and police vehicle seemed to need to drive through my school crossing patrol that morning … several times! Even Andy managed to drive over from leafy Wimbledon to have a giggle at my expense.

Despite being a laughing-stock that day, some of the most fun I have had at work has been behind the wheel of a police car. It is not to everyone's liking and some who join have no inclination to drive police cars at all. There are many who are more focused on making their way up the rank structure and possibly even reaching the heady heights of commissioner of police. But how does getting promoted in the police actually work?

CHAPTER 11

HOW CAN I GET PROMOTED?

There may well be at least one person reading this book who could eventually become commissioner of police or, as the media like to refer to the individual holding that title, 'Britain's Top Cop'. This title always seemed unfair to me as why, just by virtue of being the most senior officer in London's Metropolitan Police Service, do you immediately become the top cop in Britain? I am sure the chief constable in Manchester or Scotland would have a different view, but managing the police service in the country's capital does give the holder some distinct credibility and status. At the time of writing, there is currently an application process underway looking for the next commissioner of the Metropolitan Police. The commissioner of the Metropolitan Police is an appointment made by HM The

Queen after a recommendation from the Home Secretary and the Mayor of London. In most other police forces, the chief constable is selected and appointed by the existing Police and Crime Commissioner (PCC) for that policing area. Those working in these positions are elected for a four-year term of office and can serve two terms if re-elected. For the post of commissioner of the Metropolitan Police Service, the job description in December 2016 included the following requirements.

The successful candidate will:

- have extensive experience of leading a policing organisation, using evidence-led policing to deliver for, and with, the public;
- show evidence of successfully leading transformational change in a challenging financial climate;
- show evidence of leading outstanding delivery of effective operational policing and partnership work to reduce crime in challenging situations;
- show evidence of an understanding of changing crime and threat patterns, and the protection of the most vulnerable;
- show evidence of a lasting commitment to respecting and valuing difference and inclusion;
- have experience of working successfully with national and local Government and an understanding of the wider political, social and economic context;

- show evidence of displaying and role modelling credible, visible and empowering leadership;
- have effective interpersonal and communication skills and demonstrate sound ethical judgement;
- have a successful track record of working with diverse communities to achieve positive outcomes; and
- have a commitment to serving the public and developing excellent services and support for victims.

The advertisement went on to say that applicants should already be serving UK chief constables or have recent experience at these levels. Interestingly, it also mentioned that they would accept overseas applicants from chief officers of police. So, having looked at the requirements needed for the role of commissioner, maybe we should start by setting our career aspirations a little lower at first and looking at the normal route for promotion through the ranks.

First of all, I will describe the 'normal' route for promotion and movement up through the ranks. The recognised promotion process in policing and in most forces is now conducted under the College of Policing National Police Promotion Framework (NPPF). You will complete your two years' probationary period and then be confirmed in the rank of constable, and that may be as far as you want to progress. You can remain a constable for the remainder of your service and, regardless of how many arrests you make or how much experience you have, you will not automatically be promoted. Promotion (and salary) is not governed or influenced by the volume of work you do or the amount of policing experience you have. It is not a job where you are paid more by virtue of the number of arrests you have made or by specialising in a particular role. The rates of pay are fixed for each rank, although there may be some incremental changes determined by an individual's length of service in that particular rank. Whether you are a constable on a neighbourhood team, response team or murder investigation team, you are the same rank and receive the same rate of pay. The same goes for any specialised roles, such as firearms officers or dog handlers. Specialised roles in policing do not attract salary increases, although some will receive additional allowances depending on the role they are performing.

Once you have been confirmed in the rank of constable after your two-year probationary period, you can apply for a promotion to the rank of sergeant. This entails a four-step process:

Step One: Competence in current rank
Step Two: Legal examination
Step Three: Assessment against rank-specific competencies and
    matching to vacancies
Step Four: Temporary promotion and work-based assessment

(Taken from College of Policing National Police Promotion Framework.)

The first step is to ensure that you have been considered competent in your current rank (constable) before worrying about the assessment of your suitability for the next rank (sergeant). There is a paper application process which is submitted through a supervising line-manager, and you will need to meet certain criteria around meeting the attendance at work policy, i.e. not too many periods of sickness leave. Your performance in the constable rank will also be considered in terms of your annual appraisals and whether there have been any written or final warnings given to you. Once you receive the paper approval you then move on to step two of the application process, which is the legal exam. This is a theory-based multiple choice test on legislation and police powers. The questions are specifically directed towards knowledge of the sergeant rank and the study material available online and from various providers takes you through the enhanced knowledge you need for the next rank. I was lucky enough to pass my sergeants' theory test first time, but this required some significant studying and hours spent going through reading material and mock tests.

I decided to go for promotion when I had seventeen years of police service so although I was reasonably experienced in practical policing, the knowledge I needed for promotion was different. There were various new pieces of legislation that I needed to know very well for exam purposes that I had only a passing knowledge and practical understanding of as an operational constable. Arguably, the best time to take the sergeants' theory exam is as soon as you can after you have completed your probationary period whilst a lot of the knowledge is fresh in your mind. This slightly flies in the face of my own personal view that the best policing experience is gained from actually doing the job and the more practical exposure you can get the better. There is a balance here to be found and I would suggest possibly five years as a constable and then go for a promotion if that is your career ambition, as that would give you a good grounding in operational policing. Everyone is different, of course, and some could take the theory exam sooner or much later and still pass and be an effective sergeant. It usually takes about two years from starting the promotion process to actually achieving the next rank, and that is provided you pass each stage at the first attempt – so maybe factor that time frame into your career plan.

After the theory exam, you will move on to step three of the National Police Promotion Framework (NPPF) and this is where it becomes a bit 'grey'. The College of Policing who have devised this promotion procedure have not settled on a standardised process for this stage. Their guidelines state:

> It is the responsibility of the force's senior management, in
> conjunction with human resources specialists, to decide on

the structure and techniques to be employed in Step Three in order to select the appropriate candidates to the rank aspired to.

Forces are encouraged to utilise positive action to encourage applications from officers with protected characteristics that are under-represented in supervisory.

Forces must advertise at an early stage the method chosen to test candidates at Step Three, and the National Occupational Standards used at Step Four, to give candidates the opportunity to prepare for the process. Forces must set out the competencies they are testing and any other requirements of candidates. Candidates must be told about any changes to the advertised process as soon as possible. Advising candidates of the projected number of vacancies at a rank, and the potential numbers of candidates seeking promotion should be seen as good practice prior to the start of a Step Three process.

Where do I start? Depending on where you work, it will be down to your particular police force to decide the format of step three. I have experienced the majority of approved methods in my attempt to reach the rank of inspector in the latter part of my policing career. The methods have usually involved some form of written and practical assessment. This may comprise an interview in front of a panel where you are asked questions relating to how you would deal with supervisory related policing matters. They may ask you to give a presentation or briefing on a fictitious crime problem or community issue after you have been given a limited amount of time to read and then prepare your briefing. It may also take the form of some role-play scenarios where you perform the role of a supervisor to make sure your communication skills are suitable and competent for the role. Whatever method is chosen, it is the first practical test of your ability to perform at a supervisory level in policing.

If successful at step three, you then move on to step four. This is a mandatory twelve-month period of temporary promotion during which you are continuously assessed to see if you achieve the relevant qualifications and credit units contained in the promotion framework. Once you have successfully completed the twelve-month period of temporary promotion and have passed the qualification and attained the credit units required, you are then 'considered' for promotion to the substantive rank. This effectively means your force can then decide whether to confirm you have been promoted to the rank of sergeant. Hopefully, after all the time and effort you will have put in, your application will be successful!

The next rank up from police sergeant is that of police inspector and the application process duplicates the sergeant promotion framework. It's another four-step process with a theory exam at step two and then a local assessment at step three before the twelve-month temporary promotion at step four. During this time, an assessor is assigned to you to make sure that you meet the units or credits required as they observe you performing the role. The period of time taken before you put yourself forward for this promotion again is largely down to the individual and vacancies available in your particular police force, but you would obviously have to be confirmed in the sergeant rank first and show competency in that role before applying to be an inspector. The theory exam for the inspector promotion is harder than the sergeants' one as it combines all the knowledge expected of a constable and sergeant with understanding of all the inspector's roles and responsibilities.

On average, without any fast-track scheme, you are probably looking at about ten years of service before being promoted to be an inspector. This may sound a long time, but factor in the two-year probation period and the fact that each promotion procedure takes about two years to complete, and that accounts for six years. Two years of operational policing is a good period of time to gain the knowledge and experience sufficient to become competent. There are some who manage to find an administrative role as a constable and this allows them to study whilst at work. The same can be applicable for sergeants as well, enabling you to study whilst doing a 9–5 job, which is infinitely easier than trying to do it whilst working shifts.

I found it very hard after being on duty all night to get up late in the afternoon and then spend three or four hours studying before going back into work for another night duty. The same can be said about working earlies, which may mean that you work for eight to ten hours before going home and studying for three hours or so, if you manage not to doze off whilst reading about traffic legislation.

Taking promotion in the police service is a huge commitment both professionally and personally, as you have to dedicate yourself for a significant period of time to studying and passing the theory exam. The time for studying is often in your own time before and after work, so it can have a major impact on your personal and family life. It is designed to be hard to pass and rightly so, but there is an argument that only the more academic applicants are likely to pass as opposed to those who are effective, practical and operational police officers. Some may be excellent at exams and know the legislation back to front but on a Friday night in the high street, they are not quite as proficient in communicating or dealing with a confrontational incident as others. This problem has never really been resolved in any police promotion processes and some may not even think a problem exists. The brightest and most academic police officers will be the ones who rise to the top and in some respects that may be very welcome, as they are the ones who have to decide and form future policing strategy and objectives. I believe that there should always be a place in any promotion system where the ability and capability of an individual counts just as highly as how well they can remember policies and pass a written exam.

It really is down to you to decide how far up the promotion ladder you want to go and the type of policing work you want to experience as you do so. I will deal specifically with detectives and promotion in the CID in chapter twelve, but they also undergo similar promotion process as uniform officers.

After becoming an inspector, the next step up is chief inspector rank or, if this rank has been abolished due to cost-cutting in the force, you may have to look at options to become a superintendent. Some forces may retain chief inspectors or the role may well make a comeback if the proposed changes do not work. It is a significant jump in actual policing terms from inspector to superintendent, but for PACE authorisations it is the next step in the level of authority. At the time of writing, it is difficult to envisage what sort of method will be used to assess people wishing to be promoted from inspector to superintendent. The current method of promotion is different to that used for sergeant and inspector. Some variations may exist from force to force as it is not part of any national framework. It is solely based on a paper application form and an assessment centre day, which have to be approved and confirmed by a line-manager. The Metropolitan Police issued this timetable for the process to apply for promotion from inspector to chief inspector in 2015:

- Process launched
- Expressions of interest completed on Met HR
- Positive action intervention for application stage
- Candidate completes a chief inspector's application form
- Line-manager reviews candidate's application form and completes assessment of readiness and assessment of statement of achievement
- Chief superintendent to review the assessments of readiness and achievement.

That isn't the end ... there's more!

- Chief superintendent to forward application forms to police promotions team
- MPS central business group panel takes place
- Application form results are entered onto a spreadsheet
- Occupational psychologist analyses results and prepare options for consideration by the MPS cross business group moderation panel
- The MPS cross business group moderation panel considers the options and determines the number of candidates that will go through to the assessment centre stage

- Successful candidates are invited to attend the assessment centre

ASSESSMENT CENTRE STAGE

- Occupational psychologist analyses results and prepare options for consideration by the promotion review panel
- The MPS promotion review panel consider the options and determine the number of candidates recommended for promotion
- Posting panel process
- Top performing candidates notified of eligibility for fast-track promotion process.

So, after submitting an application form that requires approval and recommendation from your line-managers, you attend the assessment centre. If you can successfully 'sell' yourself on paper then your promotion to chief inspector or more likely superintendent is based on your performance during one day at an assessment centre. The Met also published these guidelines about assessment centres for inspectors wishing to be promoted:

> If you are invited to attend the assessment centre, you will be provided with a Candidate Preparation Pack which

will provide further details about what to expect and how
to prepare for the day. The assessment centre will consist of
the following:

- An interview. The interview will be based on the MPS
  Performance Framework (MPF), MPS Values and the
  requirements of the rank of a Chief Inspector.
- A partnership meeting exercise, designed to test skills and
  competencies considered critical to successful performance
  as a chief inspector.

The purpose of the assessment centre is to provide you with
an opportunity to elaborate on your skills and try to convince
the assessors that you are a suitable candidate for the rank of
chief inspector.

This may become historic if the chief inspector rank dis-
appears from policing, but the principle for promotion beyond
the inspector rank is likely to remain the same. Promotion from
inspector upwards will also be largely based on an application
form and then performance under assessment. The higher up
the ranks you go, the longer and more involved the assessment
process becomes. The constant theme is that it is all largely
theoretical for the higher police ranks. Currently, there is no
ongoing assessment process or probation period when you
are promoted in the higher ranks. The higher ranks do not
have the temporary promotion that sergeants and inspectors

have where they are assessed for competence. They are just successful at the assessment centre and then promoted.

It may sound strange that the operational ability of a person seeking promotion is not tested beyond the rank of inspector. It confirms my belief that from inspector upwards you are largely an administrator and business manager with very little exposure to operational policing. The main problem with police management is the lack of knowledge or expertise many of the leaders have in specialised management roles; effectively, they are police officers trying to be business managers. Police officers in general enforce the law and keep the peace but they are unlikely to be trained or experienced accountants or HR managers. If you become a chief superintendent, you are wholly responsible for the management of a very large budget and some significant HR issues to resolve. That is why policing may benefit from expertise outside the police service, as historically we have been poor at managing finances, tendering for contracts and managing personnel issues, amongst many other recognised business practices.

I could recount numerous stories about officers either performing poorly or being off sick for extended periods of time and not being managed properly by senior officers. The favoured phrase used to describe management policy has been to be 'risk averse' which means being frightened of legal action or being taken to an employment tribunal. This is largely due to lack of understanding of employment law and legislation and a general reluctance within the police service to deal with the problem. The result is they normally just fail to act and hope it will just resolve itself or even go away, and the situation is left to continue. This has an effect on morale as officers have to pick up the slack caused by absences or poor performance by a few individuals.

I can foresee in the future a greater emphasis being placed on promotion assessments for the higher ranks, testing or evaluating an individual's ability in business, financial and personnel management. In essence, from the rank of chief superintendent upwards you are similar to the chief executive of your own medium-sized business or even a fairly substantial-sized company, depending on where you are policing. Your workforce may number in the thousands and chief super-intendents are responsible for all their work-related issues, plus some personal problems as well. This role requires the very best people to perform it well, and looks for those individuals who have their officers' best interests at heart and can balance the demands of the public, as opposed to those just seeking the next rank and further promotion.

Promotion can be very rewarding and not just financially, although you will receive an increase in your salary and there are usually several annual increases based on length of service in each rank. There is clearly a greater degree of responsibility the higher up you go and a greater level of involvement in decision making. 'Role not rank' is a great phrase always used in Public Order policing circles. This means that although an individual may be of higher rank, the role held is far more important than the individual's rank.

There is a system of command and control used across the country in every police force and other emergency services for major events and incidents, called the gold, silver and bronze command system. This structure is described in a government document detailing how to deal with critical incident management:

THE COMMAND STRUCTURE

The gold (strategic), silver (tactical), bronze (operational) command structure is role based rather than grade based. Each role is allocated according to skill, expertise, location and competency.

Gold Commander

The gold commander is ultimately responsible for determining the strategy for managing an incident including any tactical parameters that the silver or bronze commanders should follow. The gold commander must retain strategic oversight of the incident. While gold should not make tactical decisions, they will be responsible for ensuring that any tactics deployed are proportionate to the risks identified, meet the objectives of the strategy and are legally compliant.

Silver Commander

Silver is responsible for producing the tactical plan following the strategy set out by gold. There can be more than one silver commander but each must have a clearly defined and logged remit.

Bronze Commander

Bronze commanders take the operational decisions necessary to accomplish silver's tactical plan. As with silver, there can be more than one bronze as long as each has a clearly defined and logged remit. For example, an incident may require a bronze operational commander, a bronze communications commander and a bronze logistics commander.

In practice this could mean that at a major incident or event, a superintendent could be gold and a chief superintendent could be a silver or bronze. In the context of the event they are dealing with, the person setting the overall strategy may be the lower-ranking police officer, the superintendent. I worked on many events where a lower-ranking officer was the event gold or silver due to their knowledge and expertise. However, this doesn't quite transfer all the way down the ranks, so you would not ordinarily have a constable or sergeant as gold or silver with a superintendent working as their bronze, as the different roles do require an element of management about them.

When it comes to promotion, you may face a long and challenging road ahead if that is your aspiration. My only advice is to try to remember what it was like for you when you first joined, along with the demands and difficulties that operational officers face. The police service needs the very best leaders who put the public and their officers ahead of their own personal goals and ambitions. I have worked for some excellent leaders in my policing career, but I have also worked under my fair share of self-obsessed and selfish individuals. They are only interested in moving up to the next rank and care nothing about who they have to push aside in order to get there, nor the problems they may leave behind them. Here's an easy piece of advice for anyone considering promotion: don't create problems just for the sake of looking good when you successfully resolve them. If a policy or system is working, then don't try to change it just to gain evidence for your own promotion application.

Promotion is not the only avenue open to you to progress your career after you complete your probationary period. There are many specialisms open to police officers and some are described in this book as a chapter in their own right.

Becoming a detective, driving police cars, working in Public Order or becoming a firearms-trained officer are all specialised roles that require specific training. There are many others including being a dog handler or joining the mounted section and in essence policing is a very wide and diverse career with many routes open to you to progress once you are confirmed in the rank after your probation. The normal process for officers is to express an interest in a particular specialism and then attend some sort of open day or maybe work with that unit for a short period of time. What your interest is and the unit you want to progress into will largely dictate how involved or how much experience you can get in their actual work. Clearly, if you want to become a firearms officer then the armed unit will not issue a gun to every officer who turns up on one of their open days. In the same way the mounted branch will not give you a horse for a day or the dog section one of their police dogs for a day at work. What you can do is attend these units and look and listen to the type of work they are involved in and learn about the selection and training requirements. During your normal police duties if the armed unit assists you at a call or incident or the dog unit helps you then watch and look at what they do. Speak to the officers, once the incident has been resolved, and mention your interest in doing that type of police work. Your general policing duties will bring you into contact with many other specialised police units and don't be afraid to express your own personal interest in doing similar work.

The rank structure has been fairly standard across all UK police forces for the last thirty to forty years.

In the county forces, the ranks are as follows:

Police constable
Police sergeant
Inspector
Chief inspector
Superintendent
Chief superintendent
Assistant chief constable
Deputy chief constable
Chief constable

In the Metropolitan Police there is a slightly different structure of ranking above chief superintendent, with the addition of the commander rank and deputy assistant commissioner rank:

Commander
Deputy assistant commander
Assistant commander
Deputy commissioner
Commissioner

You may notice that in the county forces, assistant chief constables have the same badge of rank as commanders in the Metropolitan Police and City of London Police. In the county forces, the deputy chief constable is equivalent to the deputy assistant commissioners in the Met, and chief constables are equivalent to the Met assistant commissioners. This explains the title 'Britain's Top Cop' for the Metropolitan Police Commissioner, as there is no other equivalent rank in UK policing.

Some forces have already reviewed or 'streamlined' the rank structure and, in London, the commander and chief inspector ranks are due to be phased out by summer 2018. County forces may follow suit if they have not already done so. This follows recommendations first mooted under the Sheehy report from the early '90s that police ranks that have no legal authority under the Police and Criminal Evidence Act (PACE) 1984 should be removed. Under PACE, most legal authorities that require some police supervision fall to the inspector or superintendent rank. The custody officer role falls to the sergeant rank and all other pieces of relevant PACE legislation refer to 'constable' as being empowered to do something. For anyone joining the police service in future years, the rank progression will be constable to sergeant, then inspector, then superintendent, then chief superintendent and so on. There are also some reviews underway around the chief superintendent rank as again, that has no direct responsibility under PACE and they carry out the same PACE legal authorities that superintendents do.

The other unknown in respect of promotion opportunities is the Direct Entry (DE) programme, which was designed to allow individuals with specific knowledge or experience that may benefit policing enter the service at a senior level. It is a project that has been largely pioneered and managed by the College of Policing, but it has been significantly supported and heavily encouraged by the Home Office. The intention was to attract senior managers from other areas of business to policing so that they will bring other innovative ways of thinking into a policing environment. I was not an advocate of this programme, as I still believe the best way to learn and become a leader is to work your way up and experience the job for yourself. I have slightly changed my view as I can see the benefit of recruiting some individuals whose knowledge and expertise will benefit the police service. I just do not see why they need to hold a senior police post to allow their knowledge and expertise to benefit policing. In the reality of day to day policing, superintendents are considerably removed from front-line operations and are predominantly strategic managers with responsibility for budgets and personnel matters, amongst other issues. They tend to chair meetings and meet with community leaders and politicians to discuss policing issues and rarely patrol the streets or deal with operational incidents. I accept that is a fairly broad-brush view, but if police senior officers were to be completely honest, that is what generally forms the bulk of their working day. They may well be the senior officer in charge of a sporting event or public gathering one evening or at a weekend, but the rest of the time it is largely an administrative policing role. Whilst I can see why the College identified this rank as suitable for DE applicants, in my view you cannot substitute the experience gained as an operational officer as you work your way through the ranks.

The key here for Direct Entry at any level is being very selective about picking the right people with the right skills and experience that are of benefit to the police service. I maintain, however, that Direct Entry reduces the promotion opportunities for existing officers. This could conceivably mean that experienced officers may leave the police service as opportunities to progress are reduced. I am totally against the Direct Entry programme for inspectors. This is because inspectors form the last senior police rank that is primarily operational at the front line. By 5 p.m. on any Friday anywhere in the country, most of the ranks above that of inspector have gone home for the weekend and the majority of policing areas are left under the management of a duty inspector. There will always be a senior officer available on call but the inspector is the one at any crime scene or incident who is in charge. To effectively perform as a duty inspector anywhere in the UK, you need to know and fully understand how to deal with a variety of policing incidents. The only way you can achieve that is by working your way up through the various roles and ranks and actually experiencing the responsibilities of policing for yourself. My personal opinion is that Direct Entry inspectors are a step too far in the policing world.

A popular myth, probably circulated by those in the detective branch, is that anyone moving into the Criminal Investigation Department (CID) does so on promotion. This has never been the case and detective constables and detective sergeants hold the same rank as their uniform colleagues and are on the same rate of pay. It was often referred to as moving up to the CID or 'going back to uniform', hence the misperception that working for the CID is an upward move. So, what is it actually like when you become a detective and how does it differ from the iconic 'bobby on the beat'?

CHAPTER 12

I WANT TO BE A DETECTIVE

I always ask the recruits I train 'What do you want to do in the police?' Many seem to want to be a detective, but they have a dubious perception of what the role actually entails. What does being a detective really involve? And what sort of police detective can you be? The answer from most recruits seems to depend on their viewing preferences, with their favourite TV detective providing them with a pre-conceived image of the CID. This makes sense, as most police TV shows seem to be predominantly based on detectives rather than uniform cops.

The original iconic detectives are the lollipop-chewing Theo Kojak and the 'Get yer trousers on, you're nicked!' Jack Regan from *The Sweeney*. Those characters along with many others – such as Idris Elba as Luther and the wonderful Helen

Mirren as *Prime Suspect*'s Jane Tennison – have helped form a particular perception of police detectives. The truth is, reality is very different from what you see you on a plasma 55-inch screen with surround-sound and a few hours to solve a serious crime, with the odd advertisement break for good measure. Despite my love of *The Sweeney*, I was never attracted to becoming a detective when I first joined and that view continued throughout my service. I worked a fair amount in plain clothes but never took the detective exam – yes, there is an exam to become a detective! I have written already about the significant changes in policing over the last thirty years, and it appears that the changes are not slowing down. At the time of writing, there are already plans in place to recruit police officers as detectives from the very start of their policing career so they will not work the first two years in a uniform role. The normal and recognised pathway into the CID, however, is to join as a police recruit and complete your two-year probationary period before applying to become a detective.

Despite the popularity of detectives on TV, in the last few years it seems that attracting new detectives has become a problem for the police service and there is now a significant shortage in many forces of CID officers. I find this strange as, historically, moving from uniform and front-line operational policing to a detective role has always been seen as progressing. That may not be my personal view but being a detective is, in its own right, a specialised role that requires additional studying, specific training and an examination. In basic terms, you cannot just move from being a uniformed police officer to a detective branch and automatically become a recognised detective. Being in the CID is a very different policing role than that of the iconic patrolling police officer. In the main, detectives do not patrol the streets, respond to incidents or deal with emergency calls, as they are investigators. The department was formed to investigate serious crimes, so dealing with disputes and other low-level crime is not within their operational remit.

I have my own views on why there are problems with recruiting officers into the CID in the current policing climate. Most of the classes of police recruits I have taught over the last few years have included a fair proportion of people with a keen desire to becomes detectives, so what happens once they join to cause this apparent shortage?

The current shift system for most police forces may vary from area to area, but in general it is usually three or four days on and then the other days off. Whilst on duty, you deal with the calls for police as they come in, and then the shift coming on to replace you continues with whatever incident you may be involved in. Speaking to officers working in communities and on response policing, they prefer this working environment as it gives them an element of control on their life and the unexpected nature of the day to day role makes it exciting whilst at work. In contrast, those in the CID are usually trying to manage their own huge caseloads of ongoing investigations and inquiries whilst keeping in contact with everyone involved. They have to manage the wishes and expectations of the victims and witnesses, and explain the occasionally convoluted workings of the Crown Prosecution Service and the Criminal Justice System. Once they are assigned a case or crime to investigate, it is theirs and they have all responsibility for the investigation until it is concluded.

I am told that in many places CID officers often work longer hours than their uniform counterparts, frequently having to stay much later at work to complete investigations and interviews. The delays created when dealing with detained and arrested persons during the custody process adds to the time they must spend at work. In some cases, uniformed officers may make an arrest and, after completing their arrest and incident notes, will hand over the investigation to a detective. In my experience, this did not always go well and there was often a lengthy and sometimes heated debate over who should take over responsibility for the ongoing investigation. Debate was over whether the offence was sufficiently serious to justify allocating it to a detective rather than leaving it with the arresting officer. It would appear some things have changed and dealing with victims is now a priority for police forces, which is possibly why more crimes and allegations are allocated to detectives than they were before. Whilst you might think that detectives have more time to focus on making further inquiries because they are not constantly dealing with emergency calls as their uniform colleagues will be, this is not always the case. If you factor in the increased workload for detectives with the demand on keeping victims/witnesses informed of case progression, together with longer working hours, you can start to see where the recruiting difficulty may lie.

Most detective roles are contained within what is considered to be normal working hours, which is usually from 7 a.m. until about 10 p.m. If the CID are dealing with an arrested person and waiting for solicitors or doctors to attend, their working day immediately becomes longer and sometimes they will have no idea when they are likely to finish. Community or front-line uniformed police officers are on set shifts and finish at the appointed time unless they are dealing with a specific incident. It would appear that they are the ones who achieve a greater work/life balance, but it really depends on the individual and their own personal circumstances. I know many career detectives who were glad to get out of uniform after their two-year probation and into plain clothes. They enjoyed investigating crimes as well as having the responsibility for a case and taking it to its conclusion. They loathed shift work, especially having to work nights, and did not enjoy the uniform-based type of police work where you have to respond to any number of calls.

One of the most attractive aspects of being in the police for many is the wide range of diverse roles you can perform and the ability to move between different units and jobs. Detective work is certainly varied and it can be both rewarding and very interesting.

The Metropolitan Police have just introduced an entry scheme for recruits who want to join the CID which allows them to start as detectives as part of their two-year probation. In effect, you join in the usual way and undergo your initial training in London for thirteen weeks, but then you are offered in the first two weeks the option to become a detective. If you decide to take that opportunity, you must pass the exams at the first attempt during those thirteen weeks and successfully complete your initial training. This is where it differs from normal training, as you start to learn to be a detective. It was brought in as a trial scheme to try and attract officers at a very early stage to a detective-based career. There is currently nothing stopping you from moving to a uniformed role later in your career if you choose to start as a detective. You are still a fully trained police officer and can move across departments if your managers approve your request.

There are suggestions that they may expand the scheme to invite people who have been special constables for six months or more to join as prospective detectives. They will all go through the initial training, but will then start as trainee detectives as opposed to the normal probationary period of two years in uniform on the streets as a patrolling constable. My view is that the first two years are invaluable to gaining an insight into what policing is like and informing what specialised role or department you may want to work in. Whilst it is not a long period of time for anyone committing to a career as a police officer, it gives you enough time to decide what you would like to specialise in after those initial two years.

So, what kind or type of detective can you be? The CID contains a wide variety of specialised roles in its own right and has as many, if not more, different specialisms than the uniformed branch of policing. The majority of detectives work in a main CID office, dealing with major crime investigations such as robberies, serious assaults and burglaries. The distinction between a serious major crime and what can be investigated by the reporting officer is largely dependent on the circumstances and potential leads for any investigation. Detectives tend to be located at most major police stations but are not often based in smaller community police stations. Some forces may have their own dedicated robbery or burglary teams that may include some detectives, and their focus is to prevent, detect and investigate those types of crimes.

Training at the main CID office is similar to that of the two-year probation for a uniformed patrolling officer, whereby you learn about being a detective by dealing with a variety of crimes and investigations. It provides an excellent foundation for any detective before looking to specialise in the variety of roles available. Whilst working as a newly trained detective in the main office, you may be temporarily transferred to a major investigation team dealing with a serious incident such as a murder, a high risk missing person inquiry or historic allegation of crime. These squads are set up solely to deal with a specific investigation and may be large in number at the start but gradually reduce as time goes on. The Metropolitan Police still have an investigation team dealing with the murder of Stephen Lawrence in 1993 and, although it is now smaller in number and they have convicted two men of the murder, they are still actively looking for evidence against anyone else involved. There are numerous other ongoing active inquiries in the UK with detectives transferred onto them, such as the investigation into the disappearance of Ben Needham in Kos in 1991. Ben was two years old when he went missing and the investigation into his disappearance has remained active ever since, with detectives working on the inquiry and any subsequent leads. This case hit the headlines again in 2016 as an extensive search was conducted on the Greek island after new information was provided to South Yorkshire Police. The investigation team itself will have seen many changes of personnel over that period of time as detectives move on, but it remains an open investigation. It is these types of inquiries that result from a serious crime or allegation that detectives from a main CID office may well find themselves working on for a period of time. Some police forces have dedicated homicide or murder squads who are usually called in by the local senior detective or area senior police officer and take over the investigation from the local CID. They have developed a specialism in investigating murder cases and have a wealth of experience when it comes to liaising with the family, securing and producing all relevant exhibits, examining the crime forensically and carrying out sensitive witness inquiries. Murder is the most serious of offences and carrying out a thorough and professional investigation is fundamental for any police force, which is why being a murder squad detective is a highly sought-after role. The numerous TV dramas depicting murder investigations do the role some justice in many cases as it is correctly depicted as one of the most demanding roles in policing during an ongoing investigation. There is pressure from senior police officers to solve the crime and anxiety from the community, together with the desire from family and friends to get answers. It is crucial no mistakes are made or potential opportunities for finding evidence are missed, as that could significantly affect the potential conviction of the person responsible. A murder squad detective carries an enormous amount of responsibility during an investigation and these sorts of inquiries usually involve working exceptionally long hours with little sleep or time for a break. It is, however, a hugely rewarding detective role, as you are potentially responsible for identifying and convicting someone responsible for the most serious of crimes and stopping them from harming anyone else.

I mentioned a variety of roles within the CID and the list is growing longer every year to adapt as technology and crimes change in modern society. You can specialise in financial investigation as, in some cases, proceeds obtained from a crime can now be legally seized but an investigator would have to follow the money trail. This may well appeal to someone with a financial or accountancy background who understands money transfers, bacs payments and the like. Ever heard of the adage 'Crime doesn't pay'? This becomes true if a financial investigator can detect where the ill-gotten gains have been moved. To manage this line of work, you need the knowledge of an investigator and a solid understanding of how finances work. This role has developed over the last twenty years and is a good example of how modern day policing and specifically detective work has changed with the times.

Another developing crime-trend is cyber-crime, which includes things like identity theft, online fraud and social media offences, as well as stalking, harassment or trolling. These incidents have increased as the online world develops and there is a growing demand for the police to meet the challenge of investigating allegations involving computers and online offences. The phrase 'cyber detective' may well conjure up all sorts of images in your head but this is new territory for investigative policing and requires innovative methods of detection. Understanding java script, coding, hyper protocols and even the 'dark web' and lots of other things that I personally find confusing is key to progressing with these investigations. The novelty of this type of detection seems to attract some of the newer recruits to policing. The growing use of social media and some people's belief that you can hide behind a keyboard and post all manner of offensive or threatening comments means that detectives are now faced with a variety of additional investigative avenues, including mobile phone investigation. Investigators are now able to lawfully track and identify offenders via their mobile phone or online presence. This is another fascinating role to be involved in as a detective. You are at the forefront of developing new policing skills and abilities as new methods of detection and investigation are discovered all the time.

The detectives involved in cyber-crime and financial invest-igation may work in dedicated units. I know that some larger force areas may have one or two detectives trained in these specialisms who will be based in a main CID office to help deal with local crime enquiries.

The other major area involving detectives, and one that has been of the highest priority for a number of years, involves terrorism investigations. Counter-terror units now feature in many parts of the UK and work closely with the security services. For obvious reasons I will not go into too much detail about the type of work or methods involved, but it is now a fundamental part of policing. The increased threat of terrorism has seen significant surges in armed police units across the UK, and that is matched by a greater number of detectives in associated roles. The number and range of inquiries involved in counter-terror investigative work is arguably the hardest type in modern day policing. Identifying and monitoring anyone involved in planning a terrorist attack places a huge responsibility on all those in the department. The relief when detecting and preventing a potential attack cannot be underestimated but this is highly stressful work and the role requires the utmost diligence and dedication. Unlike murder investigations which look to identify the offender after the crime has been committed, counter-terror investigators also have to try to prevent the attack from happening in the first place. This role again can involve working very long hours without much warning as investigations or operations are often dictated by the actions of your suspects. Patience is a virtue in counter-terrorism work, as you have to gather information and potential evidence slowly with the intention of obtaining enough to first justify an arrest, and second to convince the CPS (Crown Prosecution Service) to charge the suspect based on what you have gathered. This work is incredibly important and recent events only go to emphasise how vital it is for safety and security.

The last specialised investigative role I want to mention is that involving sexual offences and child cruelty or abuse. Police forces across the UK have dedicated and experienced detectives working in specialised units investigating cases involving crimes such as these. They may have uniformed officers attached to them who have specific training in dealing with victims of sexual offences or child abuse and are experienced in taking the statements slowly and thoroughly. The capacity for one human being to physically or mentally harm another person just because they are able to has never ceased to horrify me. The types of offences dealt with in this area of policing are extremely distressing and it requires a very strong-minded individual to work in this role. It is very easy to say that you should not take your work home with you but that is often easier said than done. Consider for a moment that you have spent the day dealing with a rape victim or a child who has been physically or sexually abused – it is not so easy to leave that behind at work. Their faces and words may well stay with you for a long time. I never worked full time in that type of role, but I was first on scene a couple of times in situations involving rape victims and abused children and I have the utmost admiration for anyone who takes on that policing role.

One example of an experience I had was when we were called in the early hours to a woman screaming near a common in south London. We arrived on scene at about 3 a.m. with the blue lights and headlights on, and found that the screaming was coming from the front garden of a house facing the common. I can still remember pulling into the driveway of the house and my headlights picking up the image of a lone female running backwards and forwards across the front lawn clearly in a high state of anxiety. When we first took the call I had expected to turn up and find nothing, as it was not uncommon for people to call the police in the early hours to sounds of screaming and for us to discover a couple of foxes – you will be introduced to a whole new world working through the night. On this occasion, as we drove up, I had almost convinced myself it would be foxes again and that the 'ASNT' (area searched, no trace) result would be given. How wrong I was. As the woman looked towards the lights of the marked police car, she started to run towards us. I jumped straight out and started to run towards her and she immediately froze in her tracks and started screaming louder. I stopped running and slowly walked towards her and could make out the frenzied cries of 'Go away' and 'Leave me alone'. It became apparent she had been the victim of a serious assault.

By sheer fortune, I had a colleague with me who was also SOIT (Sexual Offences Investigation Trained). She quickly assessed the situation and moved in front of me as I slowly and carefully withdrew towards the car. It was evident that seeing a man approaching her, despite the fact I was in police uniform, had distressed the woman even more. Once my colleague was within touching distance of the woman I turned off the full headlights and the blue flashing light and waited by the car. It took some time and considerable compassion to calm the victim down and establish what had happened. It transpired she had been subjected to a serious sexual assault but had managed to escape from the car of her attacker near the common. My colleague quickly established the location of the assault was a ten-minute drive away and obtained a description of the attacker and his car. The victim was still too distressed for any further questions, so my colleague coaxed her to get into our car to be taken to our victim care facility. These facilities are not in police stations as it helps ensure the victims and suspects are not taken to the same location. This prevents any cross-contamination issues around forensic evidence but, just as importantly, it prevents any likelihood of them seeing each other. These facilities provide a safe and reassuring environment where the victims can be cared for and any statements or examinations can be carried out with compassion and care.

That night it was only a five-minute drive to the nearest facility, but it seemed to take for ever and the three of us travelled in silence. I dropped off my colleague and the victim and they were met by a waiting female detective. My colleague finished work about eight hours later as she stayed with the victim and started the lengthy process of obtaining a statement from her. My colleague was taken off nights and continued taking the statement until the next evening, and she was now heavily involved with assisting the detectives in gathering the evidence. She had also built up a relationship and rapport with the victim, as this is often the case in incidents like this. The suspect was, fortunately, quickly identified by corroborating evidence from a bar where they had met and mini cab records. It was swift and effective detective work and by the next evening, an arrest had been made and the suspect charged.

These are some of the exceptionally demanding roles in the world of police detectives. If you think that you may be interested in being a detective as opposed to a uniformed constable, what can you do to show an interest?

If the trial scheme that enables you to train to become a detective straight after your initial training is available in your force area, then it is very easy. You just apply in your first two weeks of your policing career and make sure you pass your exams with good marks first time to show you have the ability and aptitude. I am led to believe that the necessity of passing first time is due to the competitive nature of the application process. Anyone needing a second attempt will not be allowed to make direct entry to the CID. The more traditional or recognised route, however, will take longer, but it will give you the time and opportunity to experience different aspects of policing before committing at an early stage to one specific course. You can still show you have an interest in becoming a detective during your first two years by volunteering to investigate any offences that occur. Locate your CID office and make yourself known to an experienced detective and ask if you can assist them in any way. Ask if you can work alongside the CID for a week or more during your first two years so you can see for yourself first-hand what the daily work involves. When you report any crimes, after ensuring you have conducted a thorough scene investigation, take ownership and responsibility for the ongoing investigation. Go and ask for some help and guidance from one of the detectives and learn from them.

The last aspect of investigative work I want to cover here is the 'pseudo detectives'. These are the officers who work in plain clothes who are not fully fledged detectives. There are many roles and individual units within policing where wearing the uniform would not help their intended objective. This does not mean every non-uniform police officer is a detective, as they may just be working in plain clothes. Across forces in the UK, there may be officers working full time in surveillance teams who are engaged in specific operations against known criminals or areas where crime is prevalent. I worked on one such team in the mid-90s and trust me, trying to covertly watch someone as they commit a crime whilst wearing a police uniform is a very tough task. We worked in plain clothes in that role and set up observations around areas where criminal activity was known to be taking place. This included shopping centre car parks where vehicles were being broken into, tube stations and cash points where money was being stolen from people. None of us were detectives but we did work in plain clothes, so this may be another option for you to consider if you either do not want to remain in uniform or do not want to be a fully trained detective.

There are many officers who move away from community or response policing to a dedicated unit but do not wear a uniform and are not detectives. Specialised units, intelligence units, vice units and many others can work predominantly in plain clothes. The variety of the work and role is often attractive to many officers as they remain a uniformed officer whilst also having the opportunity of working in plain clothes for the majority of the time. They do not have to deal with endless emergency calls or guard a crime scene for hours and their work is predominantly more focused on a specific area of policing. The process for becoming one of these officers varies, and there are many informal plain clothes units or squads formed for short periods of time to deal with specific types of crime. Mostly, you can apply to join when they have a vacancy once you have completed your probation, or you may be asked to join them based on your ability or knowledge about a particular area or type of crime.

Whichever role you choose, remember that being a detective or moving into a plain clothes role is not promotion as such, although some seem to view it that way. In my view, the work of the uniformed officer patrolling communities and dealing with calls is the foundation of everything in policing. No team of investigators can effectively perform their role without the support provided by officers. The best detectives I ever worked with knew and remembered this and would often patrol with us using an unmarked car, and so were a very useful asset to have on many occasions.

One word of caution: if you ever work in plain clothes, remember one thing. If you turn up to deal with a confrontational situation, many people will not know you are a police officer. One of the main problems with officers working occasionally in plain clothes is they forget they are no longer in uniform. They know they are a police officer and they may act like one, but they are now wearing the almost trademark Superdry jacket, jeans and trainers. By turning up in similar styles of clothing and matching jackets, they often immediately stand out as police officers. They have obviously missed the point of 'plain clothes' or maybe just haven't had the 'what are you wearing?' chat the day before.

In other instances, they arrive at a call or a crime scene and start acting like a police officer but forget they are not readily identifiable or recognisable as a police officer to most people there. I have witnessed detectives or plain clothes officers being handcuffed or even struck with batons at some very violent incidents because they have not been identifiable as police. Many are now issued with very trendy looking baseball caps with 'police' emblazoned across the front to prevent this sort of confusion – and, if you are really lucky, you may even get a high-vis yellow one! All jokes aside, that feeling I mentioned earlier when you first walk out onto the streets in a police uniform never really leaves you and, as time passes, you begin to believe that people know you are a police officer every time you go out. That obviously isn't the case in reality, and for detectives or officers in plain clothes, one of the key aspects of working safely is being able to clearly identify yourself as a police officer when the need arises.

So, hopefully you will agree that detective work is a vital part of policing and that it can be a very rewarding and enjoyable part of being a police officer. Forget the TV dramas that show the lead detective doing everything from kicking down doors to car chases and then arresting the suspect at gunpoint on some windy rooftop. You may well be heavily involved in many aspects of the investigation but not every single one, as specialist teams and officers will carry out certain

I WANT TO BE A DETECTIVE

aspects of your investigation. When it comes to going for a promotion, you can take the route described elsewhere in this book as a detective. In some areas, you may move into your new promoted rank and still remain a detective. In effect, you could take the sergeants' exam as a detective constable and then, if successful, you would become a detective sergeant. Some forces may require that you transfer to a uniform post if you are promoted as a detective but that does not stop you from moving back into the CID at a later date. There are often frequent and regular moves between the uniform and detective branches of policing and some involve officers being promoted and some are just natural moves to a different unit or department.

Your career can move from side to side, depending on the type of policing work you want to do. In all roles, however, you will have to deal with some very harrowing incidents and challenging situations – so how do you go about making your first arrest and deal with your first dead body?

CHAPTER 13

THE FIRST TIME

What's it like that first time you arrest someone and say those momentous words, 'You're nicked' or maybe you stick to the correct and more accurate phrase, 'I am arresting you for…'? Ask any serving or former police officer and they will be able to tell you about their first arrest. It is a very memorable event in your policing career and something that stays with you for ever.

You will no doubt have concerns or questions about how you do it and what you have to say. These are all covered during your theory and practical training and you will be assessed as you 'arrest' one of the instructors in a training scenario. That's not real life though and, despite the efforts of your instructors, you cannot really replicate that nervousness and outright fear about making your first arrest. For most it will be something fairly commonplace or straight-forward, like a drunk or a shoplifter. It may be that other officers are already on scene and have decided that the suspect needs arresting and it's an ideal one for the new officer on the team. That can just add to your nerves as you now have an audience of fully trained police officers who are likely to be your greatest critics. You will have learnt the caution off by heart and be able to recite 'You do not have to say anything but it may harm your defence if you do not mention when questioned…' and so on. It's never that easy in front of your colleagues and the public no matter how many times you may have practised at home with mum, dad or the dog! I know of several recruits who practise by arresting various items of furniture. You would not be the first or the last potential police officer to practise an arrest by 'detaining' the dishwasher.

Whatever the situation might be, just try to remain calm. The suspect is unlikely to know this is your first time unless you tell them or give them a clue. I wouldn't suggest telling the suspect, as that may well cause them to start giving you even more things to consider – like trying to run away! You would not be in this position if your instructors and supervisors did not have confidence in your ability. Remember, you are depriving someone of their liberty, so it is important it is done correctly and professionally. The most common response when you arrest anyone is 'What am I being charged with or what's the charge officer?' At this stage they are not charged with anything, just detained for the matter to be investigated. Make sure you have established what has happened and be clear in your own mind that there is an offence and you have a lawful power of arrest. Legally, there are certain things you must comply with to make an arrest lawful and these include telling the detained person the offence they are being arrested for, the grounds for that arrest and the reason they are being detained. These requirements come from Section 28 of the Police and Criminal Evidence Act 1984.

You will have practised it endlessly in a classroom and no doubt in your kitchen but remember, if you start to stumble over the caution, it is written in the back of your pocket notebook, just take it out and read it like it is an official announcement. Take your time and slowly explain the facts to the suspect and, most importantly, take hold of their arm so they realise they are being lawfully detained. You are exercising a lawful power of arrest and detention and your suspect needs to be made aware of this. It will feel strange and almost like an out of body experience as you hear the words coming out of your mouth. Does it feel good or powerful? Is there some kind of adrenalin rush? I have been asked all these questions and many more and in truth it didn't feel like much at all to me. It was just another necessary aspect of the job I was doing.

There were no real feelings attached to it, although catching a burglar in a house or arresting someone who has just robbed a person of their wallet does give you a feeling of immense achievement. A sort of police-type legal high.

My first arrest was for affray. Before 1986, this was a common law offence and required three or more persons to be involved in some sort of fighting or physical violence. The Public Order Act of 1986 changed the legal definition of affray from a large fight requiring three people or more to just one person using violence, so in 1980 it was treated as a much more serious matter and a major crime. I joined the police aged eighteen-and-a-half and had finished my initial training before my nineteenth birthday. In those days you were not permitted to patrol the streets until you were nineteen, so every former police cadet faced a month or two employed on station duties. It does beg the question why we were allowed to join aged eighteen but, as you will come to realise, common sense rarely applies to police internal policy decisions. I had arrived at Tooting Police station in January 1980, two months before my birthday, and faced the time before I turned nineteen working on various duties inside the station. In February 1980, my team inspector decided to let me have a couple of nights out in one of the panda cars to alleviate my obvious boredom. We used to work seven nights in a row, starting on a Monday night and finishing on a Sunday night, so he decreed I could be posted onto one of the panda cars when we reached the Saturday night of that week.

I was posted onto Whiskey Delta 42 with Claire as my driver for the night. We were in Tooting High Street and, as we approached the junction with Sellincourt Road, I saw a large group of young men in the middle of the road and punches were being thrown. At the same time, I heard a call come over the radio about a large fight at the very same junction. Claire put the message out that we were right on scene. As she slowed our car down, I jumped out and without thinking ran towards the largest group shouting, 'Police, stop!' Not very imaginative I'll admit, but this was my first time! One of the men, who I could see was throwing several punches at another male in the doorway of a flat, looked towards me and started to run away. A short foot-chase later and I caught him within a few hundred yards and walked him back towards our car. Other units were now arriving, including police units from neighbouring areas as this had been a fairly large-scale fight and Claire had called for 'urgent assistance' when we first arrived. Any call for 'urgent assistance' usually causes officers to drop whatever they are doing and rush to their colleagues' aid. It is possibly the most urgent call a police officer can put out and should not be done lightly, but must be reacted to every time. I recognised colleagues from Wimbledon and Wandsworth now arriving on scene and the seriousness of the incident started to dawn on me.

I had a tight hold of the would-be street fighter and walked him towards one of the station vans that were now on scene. We had barely spoken to each other aside from me telling him he was nicked for affray. Not quite the textbook-approved method, although I did remember to caution him as we walked back and made a mental note of the time. As I mentioned earlier, we had no handcuffs in those days as they were not personal issue and there was only one set which was kept in the one area car for our borough. I was fully aware that if you lost a prisoner, it was a discipline offence and usually attracted a penalty fine of three days' pay. I tightened my grip on his arm and was keen not to lose him (or any pay!) due to my nervousness. I realised this was my first ever prisoner on my first night out on the streets and my first proper disorder call. All those training scenarios around shoplifters or drunks, and here was I with a prisoner for affray from a serious incident. I thought that every night duty was like this and that I would never be bored … how very wrong I was! I soon discovered that after midnight most of London fell asleep and the hours until 6 a.m. ticked by very slowly.

I think we arrested five or six men that night. There had been an eighteenth birthday party for the daughter of the family living above the corner shop and this group had tried to gate-crash the party. The fight was with the family members trying to stop them. The rest of my night was spent writing notes with other officers as this was a serious offence and a major incident. The investigation was taken over by our CID and some months later I gave evidence at Kingston Crown Court and all those involved were convicted.

Claire had been brilliant throughout the incident, giving an accurate assessment of the situation as we first arrived on scene and sending someone to assist me in my foot-chase. For me, it was a very memorable first arrest. It was quickly followed once I reached nineteen by three or four shoplifters and a couple of drunks, just to add a sense of realism to policing as a new probationer.

It doesn't matter what your first arrest is, you will still be nervous and the hard part isn't just the procedure on the street and dealing with the suspect. After you have remembered to give the caution, reasons and grounds for arrest, you then have to decide whether to search the detained person and if you should handcuff them. You must make sure you get the handcuffing procedure right, checking the cuffs for tightness and then double locking them before searching the van prior to placing your detained person inside it. Having worked your way through that side of an arrest, then you come to the really challenging test: presenting your prisoner to a custody officer. There may be a wait outside the custody office as other prisoners are booked in. In this case, you may have to wait inside the van in the caged area, or your police station may have a secure caged area on the ramp leading to the custody suite or just inside the outer doors. Whatever the set-up, you will remain with your prisoner until there is a custody officer available for you and then you walk the detained person into the custody suite. That title doesn't explain the room very well: use the word suite and most people imagine a plush, well-decorated and fairly large room. These suites are not like that and usually have a fixed bench opposite or adjacent to the raised desk area where the custody officer works. They are modestly decorated with grey lino-type flooring and an alarm strip running around the whole area at chest height. There is a line marked on the floor like the sort used at passport control at airports where you stand alongside your prisoner and you then relate the circumstances of the arrest to the sergeant. Custody officers are sergeant rank in the police and it is a legal requirement of the Police and Criminal Evidence Act 1984 that, in most cases, a person's detention is authorised by a substantive police sergeant.

Having entered the custody suite, you then stand with your prisoner by the line on the floor and give the circumstances of the arrest to the custody officer who will decide if the arrest is lawful and if the arrested person needs to be detained. This is called the 'ROAST' procedure and, as ever, this is a mnemonic to help officers remember what they need to explain to the custody sergeant. It stands for reason for arrest, offence arrested for, allegation, summary and times.

You then explain your reasons for arresting this individual, the offence you have arrested them for, the allegation that was made and a summary of what has been said and done. Finally, any relevant times are given, including the time of arrest and caution and the time of arrival at the police station. This is possibly the most daunting part for new officers, as they need to convince an experienced supervisory police officer they have acted lawfully and correctly and that there is a real need for this person to be detained. Modern policing now has many different methods of dealing with offences. These are more commonly called 'disposal' methods for offences. You can issue fixed penalty notices for many offences, which means that a detainee is given an instant fine for minor transgressions and there is then no need for a court appearance unless they dispute the facts. There are also postal requisitioning and postal charging methods for summary offences. These are relatively new and come from Section 29 and Section 30 of the Criminal Justice Act 2003. They came into force in 2011 after several forces trialled this disposal method and showed some offences to be dealt with far quicker by issuing summonses by post.

The new disposal methods are designed to reduce the number of people that need to be arrested and then detained at a police station. When it comes to your first arrest, you will have already decided that the matter you are dealing with cannot be dealt with in any other way than arrest and detention at a police station. If you give your ROAST information correctly and accurately, the custody sergeant will then authorise the detention of your prisoner. The same advice and guidance applies in the custody suite as it does on the street: take your time as you try to work your way through the information required in your head. You will have been assessed when giving the ROAST details in a practical scenario during your training to an experienced instructor, so you know you can do it. Custody sergeants have a certain reputation of being hard task masters, but they have a legal duty to perform and if they wrongly authorise detention then they are the ones held to account for it. They are legally obliged to be impartial in this process and cannot give you any help or guidance, so you must know your powers and the offence you have arrested for and your reasons. Once you have 'roasted' your prisoner, they are then searched to list all their belongings but this aspect is authorised by the custody sergeant. The custody sergeant is now responsible for the welfare of the arrested person all the time they are detained at that police station. The custody officer is the decision-maker in terms of your prisoner once they have authorised detention and you will follow their instructions and guidance.

Once your prisoner has been booked in, all their details have been recorded by the custody officer and they have been searched and their personal property listed, you will then place them in one of the cells as directed by the custody staff. You check the cell first to make sure it is clean and tidy and appropriately furnished. There should be a mattress, blanket and pillow available for them to use. Once your prisoner is in their cell, you can go off and start writing your evidential statement from any notes that you made at the scene. Depending on the type of offence they have been arrested for, you may also need to interview your suspect. In some cases, the interview will need to be conducted by a detective. It is also possible that you may need to compile a comprehensive hand-over file, which requires all the facts of the incident together with your comprehensive arrest notes so that another officer can pick up your hand-over file and know as much about the incident as you do. This is particularly pertinent if your prisoner is considered unfit for interview for a few hours, such as if the detainee is drunk or over-exhausted. For example, if you were to arrest someone at 2 a.m. outside a nightclub after they have been at work all day, it would not be fair or proportionate to interview them at 4 a.m. They are highly likely to be tired and inebriated, and the guidelines for interviews of suspects prevent police conducting interviews in such a situation unless there are urgent reasons. The guidelines for detention and interviewing suspects are in code C of the PACE codes of practice and in relation to rest periods say the following:

12.2 Except as below, in any period of twenty-four hours a detainee must be allowed a continuous period of at least eight hours for rest, free from questioning, travel or any interruption in connection with the investigation concerned. This period should normally be at night or other appropriate time which takes account of when the detainee last slept or rested. If a detainee is arrested at a police station after going there voluntarily, the period of twenty-four hours runs from the time of their arrest and not the time of arrival at the police station. The period may not be interrupted or delayed, except:

(a) When there are reasonable grounds for believing not delaying or interrupting the period would:

   (i) involve a risk of harm to people or serious loss of, or damage to, property;

   (ii) delay unnecessarily the person's release from custody; or

   (iii) otherwise prejudice the outcome of the invest-igation;

(b) at the request of the detainee, their appropriate adult or legal representative;

(c) when a delay or interruption is necessary in order to:

   (i) comply with the legal obligations and duties arising under Section 15; or

(ii) to take action required under Section 9 or in accordance with medical advice.

If the period is interrupted in accordance with (a), a fresh period must be allowed. Interruptions under (b) and (c) do not require a fresh period to be allowed.

You can see these are strict guidelines, and so when dealing with a detained person and maybe your first prisoner, it may not be possible for you complete the investigation of the allegation. You may need to create a hand-over file for another officer to conduct the interview.

That's your first arrest covered from start to finish. It could take you just a few hours or possibly your whole shift, depending where you work and how busy it is. Some custody suites have been known to have several hours' waiting time to book prisoners in, and so you wait either in the van or in the secure caged area with your prisoner. You are not allowed to investigate the offence at this stage or to ask them any questions about the incident. Any interviews must be done correctly with a tape recorder in an interview room. There are numerous forms and paperwork to fill in for each detained person and you may well have to wait hours for other agencies to attend your station. If your detainee wants a solicitor then you will have to wait for them to arrive before you can conduct any interview. They are also permitted to have a consultation period as well. Your detainee may need someone to act as an appropriate adult for them and all under-seventeen juveniles arrested get these as standard procedure, but some adults need them as well. The appropriate adult has an important role to play, as they ensure the detained person understands what is happening to them and why. There may also be a need for an interpreter to be present and, with the multi-cultural society we now live in, the demand for interpreters is increasing. Lastly, your detainee – and maybe even you – may need to be examined by a doctor before any interview can take place. The prisoner will always be examined by a police-approved doctor if they are taking any medication or suffering from injury or illness.

Collectively, any one of these available options could cause a significant delay in your dealing with the prisoner. You may have to wait hours for a solicitor or a doctor or someone to act as an appropriate adult. Whatever the circumstances of the incident, arrests are never a quickly dealt-with part of policing. Patience is a virtue you will most definitely acquire as a police officer if you do not already possess it, as you really cannot speed these things up.

Whilst it is not such an easy task to arrest someone, it is definitely something you will have to master as it is a key part of being a police officer.

There will be many other firsts for you as you progress in a policing career. One of the other major significant firsts, and the one that probably causes even more anxiety than arrests, is dealing with your first dead body. Obviously, any suspicious death is investigated by police but it comes as a surprise to many new recruits to discover that non-suspicious deaths are also reported by police. We have a duty to report all deaths to the coroner and, as a new probationary police officer, you will inevitably be sent to report any 'sudden deaths'. Many people will have never seen a dead body before but part of the investigative process for police is to examine and be satisfied that there are no suspicious circumstances. This means that a police officer will have to check every dead body they are called to for any suspicious marks or injuries. This does mean you have to touch the body and look at it very carefully, but you are not expected to be some sort of forensic examiner at this stage.

Your role as ever is to be an investigator and establish the facts by asking the right questions and gathering the information. Has the person been ill for a period of time? When were they last seen? Are they on any medication and, if so, what is it and what for? You should take possession of any bottles of tablets even if they are empty, as you are now acting on behalf of the coroner who will definitely want to know these facts. Once you have gathered enough information, you should be in a position to assess whether this death is suspicious or not. To confirm that assessment, the final part of your investigation must be to check the actual body – and this is where some police recruits face difficulty. For many people, death is a taboo subject and they recoil at the thought of being near, let alone actually touching, a dead body. You cannot train for this and, although some police training may include an organised visit to a mortuary, this does not seem to be compulsory. The first time you see a dead body may be when you are called to a sudden death at an address. Remember you may well arrive and find relatives or friends already on scene and they will be looking to you to take control and be professional. They may be completely unsure of why police need to attend when their much-loved friend or family member has succumbed to a long-term illness. It largely depends on whether a doctor is prepared to issue a death certificate which legally confirms the cause of death. If the doctor is prepared to do this then any police involvement can end there, but if no death certificate is issued then the death must be reported to the coroner and investigated. It is this investigation that police carry out and report to the coroner so they can legally determine the cause of death. It will not be left solely to your decision to determine whether the cause of death is suspicious and, if you have any concerns, experienced detectives or a supervisor will attend. They will assess the information you have gathered and then conduct their own examination to confirm your suspicions or decide whether the death is non-suspicious and no further detailed police investigation is required at this stage.

This is a challenging first for many in a policing career and, whereas an arrest is probably viewed as a positive aspect and something many look forward to, dealing with your first dead body is one first that many would gladly avoid. In any event, you are highly likely to have to deal with quite a few of both in your policing career and each one will be different and bring its own challenges to you personally and professionally.

CHAPTER 14

WHAT ARE THE WORST THINGS

ABOUT POLICING?

This could easily become a complete book in its own right! Although dealing with dead bodies may be one of the worst things for some police officers, there are many other difficult parts of the job. Some are not quite as obvious and are more wide-ranging to the service as a whole. I would say that one of the worst aspects about being a police officer is the far-too-frequent negative stories about policing in the media. These stories make sweeping generalisations that suggest all officers are the same. Any organisation with over 150,000 staff – and that figure does not include the support staff – will always have its fair share of transgressors and wrongdoers. No right-minded police officer wants these people working alongside them but, in my experience, they are the minority and certainly do not represent the police service as a whole. Any story involving bad behaviour by a serving or even former police officer makes headline news and, to an extent, I can understand that aspect of reporting by certain sections of the media. That these individuals are seen as representative of the police as a whole is wrong and hugely damaging to the service. Having to constantly justify yourself is definitely one of the worst parts of the job. Police officers are not all the same and if you looked into many other professions you would find examples of poor behaviour, lax judgement and, on occasions, criminal offences; but no other occupation is subject to the same sweeping generalisations as policing.

Errors can be made and police officers are human beings with the same personal issues to deal with as everyone else. Whilst everyone must behave professionally at work, police officers are required to maintain exemplary conduct when they are off-duty or even when no longer working for the force. Headlines often include 'former cop' or 'ex officer' to attract your attention. The mere fact that the individual once held the title of constable for a period of time is used to sensationalise the story and accredit similar behaviour to those still serving. When a police officer makes a mistake at work it is almost customary for many to demand that they should be immediately dismissed without any knowledge of the facts or background. By all means, we should expect the highest standards of conduct and behaviour from the police service, but everyone is entitled to a fair trial and to be viewed innocent until proven guilty, and guilt is not decided by virtue of opinions on social media.

The almost constant public criticism of policing can be very tough to deal with. So how do you deal with the criticism? There's only one way really, and that is to remain professional, continue to do the job to the best of your ability and do not react to the inevitable comparisons and flippant remarks. Try to politely explain that not every officer is the same. If possible, you could even go on and maybe explain some of the difficulties in policing if your critic is willing to listen. The bottom line is that there are many in society far too willing and ready to criticise the police but they rarely have a solution for whatever incident is being discussed. Some people will never change their view and just want to criticise, and they are usually part of the problem and not the solution. You will receive training about being balanced and fair to everyone, including those that are so quick to criticise. Quite often, these people are disarmed by a friendly and reasonable response. They are more likely trying to initiate an angry reply from you to justify their opinion about police officers, so anything that contradicts that belief or expectation is a much better result. I am not suggesting that you will ever change their mind, but you may give them an alternative view from at least one reasonable police officer.

One of the worst aspects of any job is receiving criticism from those you are trying to help. We like to think that if criticism is unjust then our bosses will support us and maybe even speak out on our behalf. This leadership quality, however, appears to have been missed out in most police management training courses in recent years, together with the bit about valuing your staff. It is bad enough when you see your profession being criticised widely in the media, but it makes it worse when your superiors don't stick up for you. Everyone is entitled to respond to complaints by giving their side of the story, but that does not seem to apply in policing. One of the worst things about being a police officer isn't just the criticism but the resounding silence from anyone in leadership roles. There are a few figures in authority in the police who are happy to give media interviews to answer legitimate criticism, and this is going some way to help, but more needs to be done to refute the lazy criticism so often levelled against the police.

During the last eight years of my career in the force, I dealt with many prominent protest groups. I policed some very committed individuals who regularly demonstrated against a variety of issues and predominantly believed that all police officers were agents of the state, solely employed to oppress the general public and subdue any dissenting voices. They considered all police officers to be the enemy and would never ask for any help or assistance at all. The main characters and regular attendees at events loved to hate any police on their protests and demonstrations.

I got to know many characters quite well whilst policing football risk-groups; and specifically those who follow Chelsea FC. Our normal working day involved locating prominent-risk fans – those historically called 'hooligans' – and then observing them in a bid to prevent them engaging in criminal disorder. During one memorable game against Manchester United at Stamford Bridge, our prominent group was in a pub quite close to Fulham Broadway underground station. As kick-off approached, they left the pub and made their way to the ground; all the while being followed by myself and our football liaison officer. Just as one of the more well-known high-risk fans entered the concourse, he suddenly kicked out at a passing Manchester United fan. The kick knocked the man to the ground. I immediately grabbed hold of our suspect and arrested him for assault, whilst other officers came to our aid to prevent the incident escalating any more aggression between the two sets of supporters. Back at the police station, the assailant was booked in and place in a cell to await being charged. I then took a cup of tea and a daily paper to his cell, much to the astonishment of my colleagues. They questioned what I was doing, but despite the fact he had committed an offence, he still deserved being treated with respect and some consideration. That is the crux of the whole matter in policing: be reasonable, fair and human, and if you see or hear something unfair, even if it is by a colleague, then do something about it.

I am always asked 'What's the worst thing you have ever dealt with?' In truth, that's quite a difficult question to answer. My 'worst' may be something you see as quite tame and, conversely, I have probably dealt with incidents that I consider normal for policing but you may well cringe at them. I normally go all the way back to 1983 when I was a young PC in south-west London and had to deal with a suicide. I was early turn and was due to be finishing around midday as our station football team had a cup game that afternoon. We were playing away in Chigwell in Essex and the journey would take us a good couple of hours. I had just finished my morning refreshments when a call came in about a suspected suicide in Balham. I set off on my own in the patrol car and was met by the fire brigade and an ambulance when I arrived at the address. A woman had poured petrol over herself and set herself on fire. She was now dead on her living room floor and, to complicate matters, she was wearing a nylon coat that had melted over her and into the floor. She lived alone and so we had to track down next of kin and notify the coroner's officer to arrange for the body to be removed, which all took some time. It's strange how one specific incident can stay with you. The image of her lying on her back with her burnt and charred clothing all around her is one I can still see. I remained at the premises until the body was removed and then we secured the house, as the fire brigade had forced entry in an attempt to save her and extinguish the fire. I went in to auto-pilot mode as I travelled to the football match on the underground and eventually got onto the pitch as a second-half sub. It was only after the game when we drove back across London that I started to really think about what I had dealt with that day. The woman was so depressed and had lost all hope that she deliberately poured petrol over herself and set herself alight. I have dealt with many suicides during my policing career but the thought of intentionally burning yourself to death is horrific. The fact I had to watch as she was finally removed was one of the worst moments of my early career. Whilst there have been others that had just as significant an impact on me, I think you do become immune and hardened as you progress through your policing career. This goes some way to explain why the majority of my 'worst incidents' come from my first ten years of policing, although I did deal with some equally traumatic incidents later in my career.

Another terrible incident I had to deal with occurred in the '80s and it concerned a case of SUID, which stands for sudden unexplained infant death. It was around 1983 and in those days, the police had to attend and report any unexplained deaths that were brought into the hospital accident and emergency departments. They were succinctly called BID which was short for 'Brought in Dead'. On this occasion the BID was a baby just a few months old that had been found unresponsive in Clapham and taken to St James Hospital in Balham. The hospital called their local police and an officer had to attend the hospital and report the baby's subsequent death to the coroner after obtaining as much information as possible. This usually meant copying the information from the patient card and then examining the body either in A & E or in the morgue. The morgue was exactly as you see on TV where the fridge door is opened and the tray is rolled out for the detective to examine the body after rolling back the sheet. In those scenes there are usually several other people on hand, including the pathologist and mortuary attendant plus more detectives; but as this was at night, it was just me. This was not a job you enjoyed doing on your own, especially since the morgue at St James Hospital was in a separate building and you entered via a dark and poorly lit alleyway surrounded by overhanging trees. In the early hours it was deathly quiet, and I used to park my patrol car half-way up the alleyway and leave the main beam headlights on.

On this occasion the baby's body was still in the casualty department, so I could carry out my investigation in the main building. I then had the awful but essential job of visiting the baby's parents' home address and conducting a scene visit. In those days, the police sent a uniformed officer in a marked car to the home address unless there were any suspicious circumstances highlighted by the hospital. It is a very positive step forward that nowadays the majority of SUID cases are referred to a detective inspector and visits to the home address are carried out by specially trained officers in plain clothes and in an unmarked car. I could drive you to the address now with my eyes closed as that day is still imprinted in my mind as it was one of the most awful things I have ever had to do. I knocked on the door and, as it opened, I could see the house was full of sobbing relatives. The emotion was very raw as I apologised for disturbing them and tried my best to explain that I needed to visit the room where their baby was found. I felt truly awful as I was shown to the baby's room. The grieving father left me alone in there until I had completed my notes. Any death has to be fully reported to the coroner and I knew that they would require a thorough description of the room, including details about the bedding, heating and general surroundings. I made my notes as fully but as quickly as I could and after expressing my deep condolences and reiterating my apologies, I left. I defy anyone with an ounce of humanity to remain unmoved when dealing with an incident like this. Decades later, I can say that I will never forget a second of that awful day.

In later years, I dealt with enough numerous serious disturbances, road traffic collisions and assaults to fill another volume. The longer you work in the police, just receiving a call, even with the briefest of details, can help prepare you for what you are about to deal with and you find some inner strength before actually arriving on scene. This, however, can't be said for the times when you literally walk into a situation and you are unprepared for what you have to deal with.

This happened to me on one night duty in the early '90s when I was driving the area car along Morden Hall Park at about 4 a.m. There used to be a very large tree in the middle of the carriageway with a low wall around it. As we drew closer, I could see smoke rising from behind the tree and could make out the mangled front end of a red vehicle that had driven straight into it. The car appeared to have been coming from the direction of South Wimbledon and driving towards Sutton, and had clearly failed to negotiate the slight left-hand bend and gone straight on and into the tree. There were no other cars around and, as we pulled up, I could see the driver's side had taken the full force of the impact and the door had been pushed open slightly and buckled. My colleague ran with me over to the driver's door and it was instantly apparent that the driver was deceased but we still requested an ambulance to attend urgently. I could hear on my personal radio the station control room running a check on the car registration number through the Police National Computer to establish who and where the car was registered to. When we had first reached the car, our primary concern was establishing the injuries or any risk of fire, but as I took a closer look at the driver, I noticed his clothing looked familiar. The driver was wearing police-issue trousers and what was now a heavily bloodstained police-issue shirt.

The ambulance crew arrived a short while later and rushed him away to St Helier Hospital. He had suffered catastrophic head injuries and probable significant internal injuries despite wearing a seatbelt, but this was before airbags were introduced. After a quick search of the vehicle after the ambulance left, we found a set of police shoulder epaulettes with his station and number on them. Our control room rang his station and they confirmed the facts that the car owner was a police officer and had been returning home after night duty. It was later established that he had been allowed to go off-duty early as he was at crown court that morning so he was on way home to grab a few hours' sleep. The accident investigators concluded that he had fallen asleep at the wheel and the car had just driven straight on and into the tree in the centre of the carriageway. If he had been 6ft either side of the tree the likelihood was that he would have struck the railings or garden wall and, in all probability, would have survived. A few years later that tree was removed when the local authority improved the section of road and removed the island from the centre of the carriageway. This is one of the worst incidents I dealt with partly due to coming across it with no warning whatsoever. The fact this was also a fellow police officer who had been doing exactly the same job as me that night and had just left early because he was due at court a few hours later, means it has always greatly affected me.

You will inevitably have to deal with difficult and challenging incidents as a police officer and, although predominantly it is the front-line response teams who bear the brunt of this, other specialist units experience their fair share. Detectives investigating cases of abuse will have to listen to harrowing accounts and take witness statements from victims, and those words and stories stay with the officers for years. Police officers investigating murder cases will also experience dreadful scenes and then may have to inform relatives and stay with them as they identify the body of their loved one. Whichever role you decide to perform as a police officer, you will not be immune from dealing with some devastating situations. You will become accustomed and resilient the more you experience and the longer you remain a police officer.

CHAPTER 15

I WANT TO BE A RIOT COP

The hail of bricks, bottles and the occasional petrol bomb greeted us as we neared the junction of Coldharbour Lane in Brixton and waited for the command from our unit inspector to 'Take the junction to the right ... go!' We stayed in tight formation with nine long shields and a pair of back up officers behind each set of three. We knew we were relying on each other, perhaps for our lives.

Brixton 1981 was the most serious disorder seen on the streets of Britain and it was the first time on the UK mainland that petrol bombs were thrown. The words 'riot cop' are commonly used in the media to describe police officers deployed in full protective equipment dealing with serious disorder at football matches, protests and the like. The correct terminology in the police service is a Public Order trained officer and my baptism into this policing role came at a very early stage in my career, but it was to become the focus of my next thirty years.

The shout of 'Cordon!' came from the inspector and was repeated by the sergeants as I turned the corner, holding my long shield in front of me. I was the left-hand shield man in a group of five officers and we walked with our shields to the junction. We moved round the corner in the approved formation of three shield units, with our long shields at the front and our back-ups binding us together. At this time in 1981, the police Public Order tactics were in their infancy and the Met deployed their long shield units in three units of five officers, left-hand unit, right-hand unit and the centre unit. Each unit had three long shields with one officer on each long shield and they were completed by two back-up officers to make up the five-man unit. When deployed as a cordon, the three long shields were pushed together sideways and the two back-up officers wrapped their arms round the waists of the officers holding the long shields to make the unit compact and united. You had to have implicit trust in your team to stay together, as one weak link meant the whole unit was at risk of injury.

Police officers are deployed to Public Order incidents in units, or Police Support Units (PSUs) to give them their full title. In modern policing they are made up of one inspector who is in charge of the PSU, three sergeants and twenty-one constables, and they usually travel in three protected personnel carriers, fully marked up in police livery and equipped with blue lights and sirens. The shield units can split up and work separately as a one and six, i.e. the sergeant and six constables with the inspector in charge of all three, but they can also deploy as 1-3-18. The advanced maths students will work out that there are three missing constables. These are the nominated drivers and will normally stay with the vehicles. I seriously began to question my sanity after volunteering to be 'riot trained'. Not every police officer is Public Order trained and there are three levels of training in policing to deal with disorder. In London, every police recruit completes a two-day awareness course in Public Order tactics but this simply covers learning about crowd control tactics and does not involve defensive or offensive tactics with protective shields. These officers are then deemed to be level 3 trained and can be deployed at public events where there is no anticipated disorder, such as Trooping the Colour or some sporting events. The next level of training is the level 2 officer and they attend the Public Order training site for two days of specific training at least once every twelve months. They are issued the full Public Order personal protective equipment (PPE), consisting of protective Nato helmet with a visor, flame proof overalls, a balaclava, protected boots, padded/protected gloves, arm and leg protection, a cricket box (for the male officers) and a very large kit bag to keep it all in that is roughly the size of a small child. When kitted up, they look like a cross between Robocop and a Ninja Turtle, but without the same level of agility.

Every patrolling officer carries a pair of personal-issue handcuffs with a serial number on them that makes them unique to each officer, a personal-issue friction-lock baton which extends when racked open with a quick flick of the wrist. It returns to its normal state by forcibly striking it against something solid … and experience has found that police station walls, lockers, windows and colleagues' body parts are not solid enough. Public Order officers also have the option of carrying an acrylic baton instead of the friction-lock one, as frequent use of the friction-lock baton can cause the lock to malfunction and the baton to retract. There was a fairly famous incident involving a Territorial Support Group (TSG) unit in London who were deployed to deal with serious disorder. They decided the best tactical option to deal with a very hostile crowd was some fairly frequent baton charges together with the odd baton strike. The problem was that the charges were prematurely ended when half the officers found their batons had retracted back into the casing as the friction-lock had failed. They were left waving nothing more than a small metal handle approximately eighteen inches long, with the extendable piece going in and out like a child's toy lightsabre.

A day or so later and they were all at the clothing store signing for some shiny new long-handled acrylic batons with their friction-lock batons consigned to the bottom of their lockers. The long-handled acrylic baton comes in a variety of lengths and you can choose the length to suit yourself. It might seem logical to choose the longest one until you place it in the holder on your belt and then sit down in your police vehicle to find the end of it is jabbing into the rear of your knee. A helpful hint: select a baton that fits comfortably between the length from your hip to your knee, unless you want a permanent bruise behind one knee. I have no idea how you test this theory out as you will look very strange pushing various lengths of black tubular plastic through your belt loops and strutting around the streets, so test it out in the equipment store!

In their yearly refresher, level 2 officers attend the Public Order training centre and undergo two days of intensive training. They deal with a number of scenarios involving mock-ups of a serious disorder in a town centre. It is very realistic and other police officers play the part of rioters, but only the instructors are deemed sensible enough to throw the petrol bombs at the police. Having met and worked with many Public Order instructors, that decision has always baffled me! A flip-chart and box of crayons are usually enough to leave them scratching their shaven heads, so a glass bottle filled with highly flammable liquid always seemed a step too far.

Lovingly referred to as 'knuckle draggers', but hardly ever to their face, the instructors are very highly trained, having to undergo a gruelling training course to teach Public Order tactics. They are also used operationally and will be deployed to serious disorders as one complete unit, and use the call sign 'Griffin' in London. Never is there a more welcoming sight than that of a complete Public Order police serial made up of the Public Order instructors. Think of old stories of the cavalry coming over the hill to save you and you are almost there.

The last level of Public Order training is level 1. These officers usually form the uniformed support groups found in most forces across the country. In various parts of the UK, they are called the Tactical Support Group, Operational Support Unit or Tactical Aid Group. In London, they are called the Territorial Support Group (TSG) and were formed in 1987 after the Special Patrol Group (SPG) was disbanded. Every TSG officer undergoes Public Order training approximately every six weeks throughout the year. It is a 'must attend' day for them and more commonly referred to as a big 'T' day, short for 'big training' day. The primary role of every support group is to deal effectively with public disorder, so it is essential that they are highly trained in this area of policing and that they take the training days seriously … to a certain extent.

The Public Order instructors at the training centre are predominantly drawn from applicants from the TSG, so the monthly training sessions are very much 'poacher turned game-keeper' and akin to trying to control and teach a class of primary school children. One of the instructor's favourite warm-up sessions involved getting the whole unit, around thirty of us, to push a perfectly serviceable Land Rover around the site. This was generally felt to be a complete waste of time and energy, and was summed up by a cynical and brash northerner who announced, 'This is bollocks, how the f*** is this going to be any use in a riot?' He then led a half-hearted mutiny as the entire unit stopped and refused to push the vehicle another inch. Our instructor, resplendent in his customary tight-fitting red T-shirt and equally tight-fitting black jogging bottoms and shiny grey issue trainers, stood glaring at us with his hands on his hips and biceps bulging in time with his neck muscles.

This stand-off lasted a few minutes or so, with various threats of physical exertions and punishments to follow if we did not continue. We held our ground and even lounged on the bonnet of the vehicle. The face of the instructor was now turning different shades of red and purple as he eventually stomped off to seek additional assistance. As he turned the far corner, one bright spark jumped up and promptly produced the keys for the vehicle and started the engine up. We clambered in and on top of the vehicle and probably set a new record for how many people you can get in/on a Land Rover after managing to fit most of us on board. We drove off in pursuit of our purple-faced instructor and flew past him, waving various hand gestures in his direction! Our victory was a brief one as 'purple face' together with his new friend 'steroid man' 'beasted' us over the next few hours, with endless shield runs and scenarios thrown our way. Never upset your Public Order instructor, as their memories are larger than their muscles and they have a surprisingly encyclopaedic knowledge of painful exercises!

Every police officer can be Public Order trained, but there is a fitness test to pass and a level of ability and aptitude to meet so that the instructors are confident you will cope with the situations you are likely to face. The fitness test is similar to the one for recruits and involves the dreaded bleep test. The level required of a Public Order trained officer is higher at 6.4 as opposed to the basic recruit level of 5.4.

Back in 1981 I found myself pioneering police Public Order tactics in Brixton, but without the Robocop-style protective equipment that is now the norm and also minus some of the effective tactics that would be developed over the next thirty-five years. To say we were making it up as we went along might sound harsh on the senior officers of the day, but from behind my long plastic shield that's exactly how it felt. This level of disorder and violence was completely new to British police on the mainland, although our colleagues in Northern Ireland had experienced significant disorder for some time. In 1981 we only had long shields, so our tactics were devised solely with those in mind and were primarily defensive, or at least they were supposed to be. The shield used in London now is about 5ft 6in. long with three handles on the inside about half-way up. There is a fixed semi-circular shaped handle on the left side of the shield that you slide your left arm through and a hook style handle that you grip with your left hand. Underneath the hook handle on the right side of the shield is a second fixed ringed handle that you hold with your right hand. Effectively, you can take your right hand off and hold the shield in your left hand as you move between deployments. If you drop your left arm down alongside your body, the shield will sit horizontally adjacent to your waistline. Until recently, every Public Order officer had to complete a timed run carrying the long shield in this manner. This run was the method used to assess your fitness level and suitability to continue with the training. Those who failed to complete the run in time were left to sit and wait in the canteen until transport could be arranged to drive them back to their police station and they took no further part in the training.

This method of protecting police officers in disorder situations is steeped in history and based to some extent on the shield work of the Romans. In recent years, tactics were developed specifically on the streets of Northern Ireland by the army and Royal Ulster Constabulary to deal with the serious disorder they faced during the Troubles. They were all based on the foundation set by the Romans and their shield tactics and the philosophy of working together as a team. Not much had changed in way of protective clothing over the centuries, and there were moments in 1981 on the streets of south London that I felt my protective equipment was not much better than wearing a short skirt, sandals and a chest plate. Even the Romans' helmets were probably stronger and more resilient than ours. Unlike the Romans with their swords and spears, however, we were issued with a foot-long piece of timber. I never used my truncheon in anger as I had seen that it usually resulted in antagonising the intended recipient even further – a bit like poking an angry grizzly bear with a stick. Not that we had many angry grizzly bears in south London and I never poked one with a stick but you know what I mean, the truncheon was largely ineffective as a defensive weapon. The tactics we were using were predominantly defensive and, remember, the Romans combined their defensive shield work with offensive sword and spear advances and cavalry charges. Those options were clearly not available when policing disorder on the streets of the United Kingdom in the '80s, although the use of horses and dogs in Public Order would develop over the years. It was clear after the riots in Brixton that police tactics needed to develop and better protection was needed when dealing with serious disorders.

One of the most significant and major developments was the

introduction of round shields, more commonly referred to as short shields, which are approximately 2ft in diameter and have two handles that can be used ambidextrously. For right-handed officers there is a movable ringed handle on the left, and once again you slide your left arm through the ringed handle so it then sits on your left elbow. The second handle is on the right and is fixed and semi-circular in shape. You grip this with the fingers of your left hand so that if you let the shield go, it will hang loosely from your left elbow. This allows you to freely use your right hand to push people away with your hand or to use an approved baton strike. Many short shields are emblazoned with the word 'Police', written so that when the shield is held by a right-handed officer on their left arm, the writing is the right way up. Unfortunately, when held by a left-handed officer the shield is on their non-dominant arm, so the word is upside-down. At least 80 per cent of the population are right-handed, hence the prevalence of right-handed short shields. The introduction of short shields allowed for offensive tactics to be used as the shields are much more manoeuvrable and easier to carry and run with. Working together, a long shield unit can provide protection from missiles and airborne objects and the short shields are used to push forward and separate the crowd.

Back to Brixton in 1981. It was about 8 p.m. and dusk was falling on the streets, making visibility extremely difficult, especially from behind a Perspex shield. We moved slowly up the street with no protective equipment as such. Some units had the green ex-army Nato-style helmet with a visor. These were army surplus and the Met had acquired them as a temporary measure to provide better protection from objects thrown. They were not great but a definite improvement on the traditional police custodian helmet. The health and safety czars of today would have had a field day about our exposure as we faced a hail of bottles, bricks and petrol bombs. I had only ever faced petrol bombs during the single Public Order training day I had attended at this stage in my career. This may have been the first time that petrol bombs had been used against the police on the UK mainland, tactics which had clearly been learnt from watching the news from Northern Ireland. As we moved cautiously forward, I was aware of a camera crew from ITV News moving slowly along the pavement on my left. I was on the extreme left of the whole unit and as I looked at the camera team, I noticed that they had even less protective equipment than we did. I caught the eye of the cameraman and said, 'I wouldn't go any further mate, it's getting quite lively.' As I finished speaking, the crew took about three steps forward and 'whoosh' – a petrol bomb landed directly between me and them. It was that close that I could feel the heat from the flames as it exploded and as glass showered the bottom of my shield, I could feel pieces of broken glass under my boots. I glanced towards the spot where the crew had been, and thankfully they managed to make a very swift retreat back to the relative safety of the junction behind us.

The day itself had started so well on the Saturday, as I was out with my then-girlfriend enjoying a rare day off together. We returned to my room in the police section house in Tooting in the early evening and were planning on going out for dinner and drinks. The entrance to the section house was at the rear of the police station so conveniently I could roll out of bed at 5.30 a.m. and still be on parade by 5.55 a.m. The convenience of my living arrangement came back to bite me on this day as I was an easy option for any much-needed police reinforcements. As my girlfriend and I opened the door of the section house, we were met by the smiling sergeant, although I am not sure why he was smiling as he did not have joyful news for me. I think I was just another number and name to be ticked off his requirement list and, once done, he could go off and enjoy his Saturday evening. He told me that serious disorder was taking place in Brixton and all shield-trained officers were being called in to work, and that now included me. The section house was a handy location to gather together suitably trained officers and, remember, this was long before mobile phones or pagers so contacting off-duty officers was very difficult. The section house sergeant ticked me off on his list and it transpired it was not just shield-trained officers he was sending back to work! Anyone walking in was told to report to work and if they were not suitably trained, they would be on standby.

On reflection, as I climbed the stairs to my room on the first floor I felt I probably had the better option in being recalled to work as opposed to some of my friends who would be spending the evening sitting in the police canteen on standby. My girlfriend came upstairs with me and joined me in my slightly frantic search for a clean and passably ironed work shirt. There was a communal ironing room on the first floor but as my mum only lived a fifteen-minute drive away, I rarely ironed my own work shirts!

Some fifteen minutes later, I reported to the canteen where I met up with other officers. In this type of situation, you find yourself working alongside other police officers you rarely see at work because of the different shifts and duties carried out. This is why it is essential that any training is standardised, so that everyone knows what is expected of them in any given situation. We boarded our so-called 'green goddess' coach for the short journey across south London to Brixton. At that time, the police used purpose-built coaches to transport police officers and they were British racing-green in colour, but that was as far as their racing attributes went. I think I could have cycled to Brixton more quickly, but eventually we arrived and were quickly deployed. At that time we even had a police approved 'debussing' system that was practised at Public Order training which consisted of the entire coach leaving in a particular order. Every green coach had a set of numbers written in chalk on the roof above every seat. Your allocated seat number depended on your position in the shield formation. The most important position belonged to the individual known as the 'key man' and they always had seat number 1 next to one of the doors, and their role was to get out first and unlock the luggage compartment containing the long shields. There were two systems for leaving the coach and they were dictated by whether the key man left via the front door or the rear door and inevitably it never quite went according to plan. There was even a method of deploying 'under fire' which seemed bizarre, given that the coaches were not protected in any way and did not have reinforced windows. This formed my first experience on how to over-complicate things police-style, and that probably helped invent the 'Kiss' approach: 'Keep it simple, stupid!'

At some point, someone decided that if the coach was under fire, the safest thing to do would be for that key man to run out, unlock the compartment and then throw the long shields under the coach towards the rear where he guessed the officers were standing and waiting. What could possibly go wrong with a 5ft 6in. Perspex shield weighing about twenty pounds being launched at ankle height under a coach? As we bent down to collect our shield, the next one careered towards us so we had to jump out of the way, trying not to fall over or knock our colleagues down. If it wasn't so dangerous with bottles and bricks raining down at us it would have been hilarious. After Brixton 1981, the officers debussed away from any disorder. It would have made for a great TV show as a kind of police ten-pin bowling contest and many officers returned from deployment with a nice bruise on their shin courtesy of the key man.

This was a pivotal moment in policing history. Even now if you mention Brixton 1981 and the riots, people will remember it as a day that changed police and community relations. For me, it was a first taste of public disorder, something that would form the basis of my policing career.

I remained Public Order trained throughout my service and finished my last eight years on the Public Order Branch, working on the intelligence unit with evidence gatherers and intelligence teams. Whilst I thoroughly enjoyed that part of policing, it isn't all excitement and, in truth, disorder is always the last thing you want or need. The right to free speech is a key part of a democratic society and along with the ability to protest against injustices, needs to be defended. There must be a balance between free speech and peace without resorting to committing offences or seriously disrupting society. If you work in Public Order, you will be faced with all sorts of people and views that you are likely to disagree with and may even find distasteful or even offensive. The police service has an important role to play in balancing the right to protest and demonstrate but ensuring other sections of society can still enjoy the freedom to work and socialise. You will need a lot of tact, good humour and patience on any Public Order event, so try to avoid being robotic or dismissive. Those attending may hold alternative opinions or views to you, but they are usually keen to explain them to anyone willing to listen, and that includes police officers.

Most Public Order deployments involve spending the day in a police personnel carrier that contains eight other officers. One of the most challenging parts of these events is surviving the inevitable boredom of being on standby at some remote location for hours on end. It is usual practice for the nominated drivers to remain with the vehicle at all times, even when the rest of the team are deployed. In Welling in 1993 there was one event when that rule changed and I ended up being eternally grateful for the resilience of a short shield. The right wing British National Party (BNP) had been largely formed by defectors of the National Front (NF) and they had a bookshop in Welling. This area was historically a highly popular location for the more right-wing types. In April 1993, Stephen Lawrence was murdered just a short distance away in what has been acknowledged as being a racist attack. By October 1993, the Anti-Nazi League (ANL) and Youth Against Racism in Europe (YRE) decided to hold a protest march against this bookshop being allowed to remain open in the area. As the main march group reached the junction at the road of the bookshop, they were met by a cordon of police officers blocking their route. They were redirected from the bookshop in Upper Wickham Lane and up Lodge Hill alongside Plumstead Cemetery. This resulted in significant and sustained disorder at this junction and my TSG unit were deployed from standby in full protective equipment to assist.

I had been posted as the nominated driver for this day and was driving police personnel carrier Uniform 513 and we had the unit inspector with us whose call sign was Uniform 511. On larger events the inspector travelled with the whole unit and would position himself with one of the carriers. We were instructed to drive down from our standby position and park all the carriers in a holding area on Okehampton Crescent so that the units could then be deployed on foot. When we arrived at the holding location, there were already several TSG carriers from other units parked and we were directed to a parking space by a uniformed constable. He told us that his unit were posted to secure the parking area as they were level 3 officers and so we could deploy our whole unit, including the drivers. I quickly grabbed a short shield and put on my Public Order boots and nominated myself to be the sergeant's assistant. Our sergeant, Mark, was a calm and highly competent leader and we followed him as he quickly walked towards the junction where we could see and hear the disorder. All three units, 513, 514 and 515, were deployed to the cemetery as some elements of the march had broken through police lines and over the fences and were trying to breach the rear of the cordon at the junction.

We jogged round the back of the police cordon and entered the cemetery half-way up Lodge Hill and made our way through the graveyard back down to the corner adjacent to the disorder. There were many people already in the cemetery and a police observation post was coming under attack in the corner, so we went to assist. Our job was to sweep through the cemetery and clear it of protesters who were now using the exterior wall as cover to throw missiles at police. They were even breaking up the large capping stones on top of the brick-work and using these as missiles to throw at the police. We immediately came under fire as we approached them. I heard Andy our unit governor shout 'Spread out', and Mark indicated by waving his arms for us to fan out either side of him. Our three units were working together but we stayed alongside the officers from our own vehicle, with 513 on the left, 514 in the centre and 515 to the far right. We ran through the cemetery towards the hail of bricks being launched in our direction. Most protesters turned tail and ran. The last few remaining die-hards stood their ground until we were almost on top of them, and then they too turned and fled towards the exit and into the main march group on the road.

It was at this point that I became aware of a very heavy and loud thud against my short shield. It was so forceful that my left arm buckled and the shield slammed into my upper thigh. As I looked down, I saw a stone paving slab that was roughly the size of a basketball and wondered what sort of monster had managed to throw that. I looked to my left and saw two young men running away through the gravestones. I thought no more of it at that stage as I was running on high adrenalin. We cleared the cemetery and then re-grouped at our carrier to await our next deployment. As we ran, I started to become aware of a dull ache in my left thigh and noticed that my short shield was feeling flimsy and I could hear a flapping noise. I looked down and my shield was opening and closing as we ran as there was a large split across the entire surface and it was held together by about 5cm of plastic. I examined it more closely when I reached our carrier and the shield had virtually been split in two by the force of the blow. It wasn't until we returned to our base at Barnes and I changed out of my protective kit that I noticed a very large purple-yellow bruise on my thigh. Without the shield stopping the slab and taking the force of the blow, my leg would have been broken. It just shows that you should always have faith in your protective equipment, training, adrenalin and sheer determination to get you through.

In my opinion, Public Order policing is a specialism in its own right. If you look at the ramifications if it goes wrong, then maybe you will understand my view. Every week across the UK thousands of people attend sporting events, public festivals, concerts, demonstrations and ceremonial events. These all come under the umbrella of Public Order policing duties and this means that every event must be risk-assessed and carefully managed to ensure public safety and well-being, and any potential for crime or disorder taking place must be closely monitored. Public Order is not to everyone's taste and some prefer more investigative roles or greater involvement in their local community. As I have mentioned before, it is really up to you to decide what policing role gives you the most satisfaction and enjoyment, and fortunately there is a very wide choice for every officer.

CHAPTER 16

EXITING OR REMAINING

This is a very topical chapter title in today's climate. There is a word that emerged from the EU referendum that could equally be applied to many serving police officers after they have a few years' service. Until 2016 we had never heard of the word 'remoaners' but it developed after the referendum to describe those who wanted to remain in the EU. At the time of writing this I began to think the word 'remoaners' could be applied with a slightly different meaning to many still working in the police.

When you first join I would be willing to bet there will be quite a few police officers who will question your sanity. They will moan about the salary, service conditions, shift rota, days off being cancelled, the Crown Prosecution Service and, more significantly, the attack on their pay and pension rights. They may all remain as police officers but will have many ideas about who is to blame and what should have been done to protect their rights. The usual focus of their moaning switches equally between the current Prime Minister Theresa May who, as Home Secretary, led the changes to pay and pension rights – and the Police Federation for allowing her to do so. I should say at this point that I was a Police Federation representative for about twelve years of my service as a constable and then four years as a sergeant. This does not mean I am blinkered to the failings or inadequacies of the staff representative body of the police service because I am not, especially since I had a front row seat for many of them. The Police Federation were hampered by many aspects of the negotiations about the pay and pension changes proposed by the government and, in truth, they managed to fight off many adverse proposals, but there were always going to be some battles they could not win. The Police Federation are often referred to as 'toothless tigers', as the law prohibits them from fighting for industrial rights in the same way as every other trade union.

You should be aware that police officers are not permitted to go on strike, as it is illegal for them to take any form of industrial action. As Officers of the Crown, they are bound by the Police Act 1996 and striking would be a breach of Section 91. A criminal offence will be committed by:

- Those who cause, or attempt to cause, amongst members of the police service disaffection, and those that induce them to 'withhold their services'
- Anyone encouraging or promoting strike action
- Anyone encouraging or promoting an overtime ban (including bans on both compulsory and voluntary overtime)
- Anyone encouraging or promoting a 'work to rule' – in effect a withdrawal of goodwill; the incitement to do so by the Federation or by a member might well be viewed as causing disaffection contrary to Section 91

That rather limits any effective industrial action taken by police officers or by the Police Federation. There are other limitations on your 'rights' once you become a police officer. These include:

- Abstaining from any activity which is likely to interfere with the impartial discharge of duty, or to give the impression to the public that it may interfere
- Not wilfully refusing or neglecting to discharge any lawful debt
- Not being able to have a business interest without the consent of the appropriate disciplinary authority
- Abstaining from an 'active' role in any party politics

There is also a common law offence you need to be aware of.

It is considered a breach of conduct if an officer wilfully neglects to perform a public duty or misconducts themselves to such a degree as to amount to abuse of the public's trust without reasonable excuse or justification.

So, police officers are prevented by law from striking or withholding their services, and those promoting or encouraging any such action may be committing the offence of 'disaffection'. If you consider the history of industrial disputes and arguments over pay and conditions in other professions, it is inevitably settled after a withdrawal of labour or a total strike. On occasion, the threat of a strike has been enough to settle the dispute, usually to the benefit and satisfaction of the workforce. I am not about to debate the benefits and successes of various industrial disputes and I may be generalising about the overall outcomes but the point is that the police and our representatives and negotiators do not have these options. Police 'remoaners' would have us staying under the old pay and pension conditions and I support that view, especially since I benefitted from them. Once the issue of pensions was raised, along with the fact that people are living longer and drawing a police pension for longer, you could see there had to be a change. It is the arbitrary way in which this change was enforced that has caused so much animosity. Many officers perceive the changes made to have effectively stolen the future from many long serving officers.

New pension rules and service conditions have been introduced, and so new officers will work under those. Pensions are still good, although the basic salary does not reflect the job being done. It would appear the current government and Home Office sees fit to limit police pay and benefits, and I can only assume that is because they believe that over the last decade or two police pay had risen too high. Of course, this view is not shared within the police service and I hope the fight to increase pay and conditions will continue so that this phrase might sum it up: 'I'm paid for what I might have to do, as opposed to what I actually do each day.' Police pay seems to be measured according to the volume of crime, but the type of incidents you may have to deal with can never be truly reflected by any financial recompense. I hope the disparity between police officers' pay and that of other professions will be positively addressed soon.

The last set of limitations over your rights as a police officer concern your 'active' membership of political parties, refusing to pay lawful debts and having any outside business interests without permission. As a brief explanation, you can be a member of some political parties but not any of the more extreme groups, such as the BNP. The guidelines do allow membership of political parties but restricts what it calls 'active' membership, and the definition of that term is based on the particular activities carried out by the officer.

You are also prohibited from refusing to pay any lawful debts but this does not mean you are compelled to pay for faulty goods or services just because of your occupation. If you do end up in a dispute over payment of a debt and it results in civil court action, you are required to report the matter as soon as possible. You have the same consumer rights as every other person but the issue is any associated discredit on the police service as you are a serving officer. You could potentially be committing a discipline offence by refusing to pay if a court decides it is a lawful debt that is outstanding, but that doesn't stop you exercising your rights as a consumer solely because you are police officer.

Finally, there are restrictions on police officers having outside business interests. Any additional paid work that you want to conduct has to be submitted for approval. This does not mean you cannot still work as a plumber or electrician or use any other skill and experience you may have to run your own business. There are many police officers who successfully run a variety of businesses or they may be partners in a business venture, but it must be with the full knowledge and approval of the service. There are restrictions on the kind of business that will be approved and, obviously, anything that may conflict with or impact on your policing role could be excluded, such as running a nightclub or anything requiring alcohol licensing.

In respect of negotiating for improved pay and conditions

or defending existing contracts, the Police Federation have generally done exactly that over the years. They have historically come from a very challenging starting position due to the legal restrictions on any form of industrial action. Regardless of the perceived lack of action from the Federation against these imposed changes, I would always advocate joining a union or staff representative body. In the policing world, it is the Police Federation that best represent you, as you will always be stronger in a united group than as an individual or as part of smaller representative bodies. You may not always agree with their approach or responses, but they do represent all ranks up to inspector level across England and Wales, and it is essential that the service has an official staff voice.

You may hear that the government has stolen many officers' pensions and, in basic terms, that is not far from the truth. Officers signed onto a pension deal for thirty years and for an agreed final sum only to be forced into a change in conditions and find that they would pay more money in for less money at the end and for a longer period of time. If that happened to any other professional body or workforce, there would be a significant outcry with strikes and industrial action. I believe that over the next decade or so the pendulum will once again swing back and police pay and conditions and pensions will be improved. It has been shown across the world and during our own policing history that if you do not pay a reasonable wage to your police service, the temptation to act corruptly is increased. I can remember being told this when I was a young PC by a very wise and experienced constable who I have already mentioned earlier in this book. Dutchie told me in my first year of service that if I am ever offered a bribe to turn a blind eye or do something illegal, I need to weigh up a few things first. Unless the person is offering me over a million pounds, a get-out-of-jail guarantee and a new life somewhere exotic I should decline the offer and report it. He explained that my wages and pension earned over thirty years of policing would amount to several hundred thousand pounds so any inducement must be a significant improvement on that. There was also the fact that, if caught, I would certainly serve a considerable prison term for such an abuse of position and trust. Lastly, once I was released, I would in all probability have to start all over again and would have lost any sight of financial gain. In truth, he didn't have to convince me as it really wasn't in my nature and I had no idea if his maths were correct, but even I could work out that bribery and corruption would not be tolerated in any form.

You will certainly never become rich or make your fortune becoming a police officer unless you're one of the very lucky ones. It really is up to you as to why you want to join and what you want to do and for how long you remain a police officer. I saw it as a vocation and I was lucky enough to be able to leave after a significant policing career of over thirty years and still be young enough to work in other roles and employment. If you are joining in the current climate and are hoping to achieve maximum pension, then you are looking at something between thirty-five to forty years of policing service, and by that time you could well be at retirement age. You will receive all sorts of worldly advice from colleagues with many more years of service and they will inevitably use the phrase 'TJF' or, more recently, 'TJRF'. Even when I joined we were told 'The job's f***ed', but since I retired in 2010 and the pension changes came in, that phrase has been updated to: 'The job's really f***ed'.

There are no end-of-year financial bonuses or employee of the month competitions to win, and promotion can be a tough process as well as any form of specialism. There will be times when you consider leaving and the demands of policing both at work and on your family and social life will be immense. I cannot give you guidance or advice as to how long you should remain or when you could consider exiting the police service. I have worked with officers who have left after significant periods of service and they will tell me it was the best decision they ever made. There are others who leave after thirty years and still miss it, and wish they had stayed even longer or maybe looked into the opportunity to reduce the days they worked. Policing is one of the worst professions when it comes to investing significant periods of time and money into training their staff and then being happy for these highly trained individuals to leave after thirty years without any effort to retain them. I am still waiting for an exit interview, and from the moment I submitted my retirement papers until my last day of service I never spoke with anyone above the rank of inspector about my decision. There was no formal interview or even an informal chat over a cup of tea or across the photocopying machine in the admin office. It was just an attitude of 'Fine, thanks for your service'. The only thing missing was a request to please shut the door on your way out and don't forget to turn off the light!

Despite the restrictions and recent attacks on pay and conditions, there are still healthy numbers of people applying to become police constables. It is possible that the concept of policing as a life-long career will be reaffirmed by the requirement to work thirty-five to forty years to attain full pension rights. Many recruits are now joining in their mid- to late-twenties, so a forty-year policing career will mean retirement in their late-sixties and it is highly unlikely they will then move on to another job. Whatever works for your own personal circumstances will largely dictate and influence your ultimate decision. It will sound strange to a young twenty-something reading this that their life plans and ambitions will change over the next thirty-five to forty years. Partners and children may well come along and your whole outlook on life changes, even where you live and work may change if your partner has a job that requires them to re-locate. You may have the intention to work as a police officer in a certain part of the country for your whole career, but circumstances can change. You may have to decide to leave policing earlier than you intended or even transfer to another force in order to be promoted or to specialise.

Whatever length of career you end up having, the skills you pick up as a police officer are viewed as significant qualities in essential or desirable criteria for many jobs. Your communication skills and capacity for decision-making will have been greatly enhanced after any significant period of time as an operational police officer. Your understanding of risks and hazards and your ability to assess and deal with them will be considerable. In short, your personal attributes and ability in and around the workplace will be of major benefit to most employers due to your knowledge and experience as a police officer.

I left with no real plans and no job to do, although there were a few tentative offers and the usual, 'Ring us when you have retired and we will have something for you.' None of those resulted in anything when I eventually contacted the people involved as apparently things had changed and moved on. Many of my qualifications from my policing career were not recognised in the private sector and, although I had co-written and delivered a national training course and was qualified as a police trainer, these attributes were only recognised internally.

My trainer's qualification was only valid whilst I was a serving police officer and once I retired, I needed to gain a more widely recognised teaching qualification. I had to fund my teacher's training course and attend a college for the first time to be officially qualified. This enabled me to teach prospective police officers and deliver lessons on subjects I had spent over thirty years experiencing for real and dealing with. It did seem rather strange that anyone with a teaching qualification would be allowed to teach prospective police officers a lesson on theft or Public Order, yet my thirty years of experience of those subjects was not sufficient. I am therefore fully supportive of any plans to recognise the profession of policing with suitable educational qualifications as a degree in itself.

This does not mean you need a degree to be a police officer or that the entry exams will be increased to be of degree level standard. My understanding is, and the explanation from the College of Policing clearly states, that the proposals are to fully recognise the knowledge and experience a police officer has, and to provide opportunities for officers to gain a publicly recognised qualification for their skills. It always seemed a bizarre situation that after thirty years of policing, you leave with a certificate of service that simply states how long you worked for. There are no skill- or experience-related qualifications or certificates that can be handed to any future employer to confirm that you can drive, ride a horse, train a dog or any other specialism you can think of. The police service places great weight on training, but does this level of attainment and knowledge evaporate as soon as you leave policing?

Of course it doesn't, and my driving skill and ability was improved and enhanced by the numerous courses I attended and the instruction I received, plus the hundreds of hours and thousands of miles driving a marked police car. You will attend and hopefully pass many similar courses from driving to interviewing and it is right that there should be some accredited and recognised educational qualification you receive that remains with you and doesn't disappear just because you hand in your warrant card. I would always recommend attending as many training courses as you can and acquiring as much knowledge and expertise from the wide-ranging opportunities that policing will offer you. Whether you stay in the police service for thirty to forty years is largely your choice but it may be influenced by personal or domestic circumstances or a better career or financial opportunity that may arise. Despite a long or short policing career, you will inevitably gain essential knowledge and experience that will be of use to you personally and, probably, professionally as well.

I currently work as a policing analyst and commentator on Sky News where I frequently give my views and assessment of a policing story or incident. I have never received any formal training or instruction in media interviews and never gave public briefings to the media when I was a serving officer. Some may say looking at some of my interviews that I am stating the obvious here but my experiences in policing and the communication skills I have acquired over the years have helped. When you have been cross-examined in the witness box for hours at the Old Bailey by a very well-educated barrister, chatting about policing on TV doesn't seem so intimidating. I heard once that being a police officer was like being the 'jack of all trades and master of none', and that is quite an apt description. I would not consider myself as a master at anything, but so far since retiring, my career in the police has enabled me to work as a driving assessor, teacher, media commentator, security consultant and tour guide. Not bad for a young man from a so-called 'broken home' in south London with no more than a comprehensive education and only four O-levels under my belt.

Policing is your opportunity to make a difference in the community you live in and to create the society you want to be part of. Policing gives you the chance to make real changes and to make people feel safer and more secure. Just remember, always be aware and observant; keep an open mind at every call you attend; and finally, but most importantly, stay safe.